SALES MANAGER'S MODEL LETTER DESK BOOK

Second Edition

SALES MANAGER'S MODEL LETTER DESK BOOK

Second Edition

Hal Fahner
and
Morris E. Miller

PRENTICE HALL
Englewood Cliffs, New Jersey 07632

Prentice-Hall International, (UK) Limited, *London*
Prentice-Hall of Australia, Pty. Limited, *Sydney*
Prentice-Hall Canada, Inc., *Toronto*
Prentice-Hall Hispanoamericana, S.A., *Mexico*
Prentice-Hall of India Private Ltd., *New Delhi*
Prentice-Hall of Japan, Inc., *Tokyo*
Simon & Schuster Asia Pte. Ltd., *Singapore*
Editora Prentice-Hall do Brasil Ltda., *Rio de Janeiro*

© 1988 *by*

PRENTICE-HALL, INC.

Englewood Cliffs, N.J.

10 9 8 7 6 5 4 3

LIBRARY OF CONGRESS
Library of Congress Cataloging-in-Publication Data

Fahner, Hal.
    Sales manager's model letter desk book/Hal Fahner and Morris E.
Miller.—2nd ed.
      p. cm.
    ISBN 0-13-787789-7 : $39.95
    1. Sales letters. 2. Commercial correspondence.   I. Miller,
Morris E.   II. Title.
HF5730.F34 1988
658.8′1—dc19   88-2537
                                               CIP

ISBN 0-13-787789-7

PRENTICE HALL
BUSINESS & PROFESSIONAL DIVISION
A division of Simon & Schuster
Englewood Cliffs, New Jersey 07632

Printed in the United States of America

CONTRIBUTORS

HOW THIS BOOK WILL HELP YOU WRITE LETTERS THAT GET ACTION

Over the past ten years, literally thousands of sales managers have used the first edition of this book to save time and improve the results of their written communication.

This week you will probably personally spend several hours working on and worrying over the right words for letters and memos to your salespeople and customers. How many hours will you spend today? Right now, do you have a letter that you would just as soon not have to write?

This second edition contains the best letters from the first edition, plus over 100 new letters, alternate phrases, and memos — for a total of 375. We have all new letters contributed by an additional 12 sales /marketing executives from some of the world's largest companies, as well as small and medium-size companies. Contributions have come from all types of sales organizations — those selling industrial goods, consumer goods, and services. They represent manufacturers, distributers, dealers, and retailers.

The letters provided in this book have produced results for you. One sales manager submitted a recruiting letter to us and penciled in at the bottom of it that one of four prospects receiving the letter responded. Contributors reported that their letters had made such favorable impressions that customers returned them with appreciative comments penned at the bottom. The letters that have won their way into this book are tested, proven ones. The contributing sales managers who share these letters with you do so because of their pride in them and the results they achieved.

A sales manager's effectiveness increases or decreases in proportion to the support and cooperation he or she receives from corporation support functions, as well as the effectiveness of the sales force and communication with customers. Sometimes the most difficult communication is with peers and staff support. The memo has become an art form in the modern business world. Chapter 8 will be your guide through ground rules and protocol. The guidelines and model memos provided will enable you to avoid the pitfalls of intercompany communication which can severely damage a career. Your memos will produce action and will build your reputation for getting things done when you follow the guidelines provided in this book.

The toughest letter writing situations are covered. Do you have to reduce your best salesperson's territory? Run, don't walk, to Chapter 4. Have to say "No" to one of your best customers who is requesting special terms? The answer is in Chapter 14. One of your service people insulted a customer? You'll find help in Chapter 16.

You will find the model letters you need to handle almost every conceivable situation — letters for salespeople, letters for customers, letters for collecting past due accounts, letters that turn complaints into additional business, letters that get action from sales contests . . . and hundreds of others.

You will find hundreds of ideas for making your everyday letters more productive. Have you ever seen sales force productivity drop after a sales contest? The ideas in Chapter 1 will keep them producing.

You will want to keep this book of Model Letters on your desk within easy reach. Imagine the ease of turning to a model letter, checking off a paragraph or alternate phrase, and instructing your secretary to include it in your letter for just the right effect.

Every letter provided here is ready to use. We have made them even more usable by providing suggestions for alternate wording to meet the variety of needs you might encounter. We have removed the technical information that was contained in the original letters so they could be applied by you more easily and rapidly. The result is a functional, practical, and valuable reference tool that will save you time and effort and will improve your letter writing results.

Hal Fahner
Morris E. Miller

TABLE OF CONTENTS

1

LETTERS THAT PROD YOUR SALESPEOPLE TO A SECOND EFFORT

1

LETTERS THAT PROD YOUR SALESPEOPLE TO A SECOND EFFORT

Have you ever noticed that a sales slump often follows closely behind an exceptional sales achievement? Why is it that salespeople can't consistently achieve the outstanding? Every sales manager has seen it happen. The salesperson makes an important sale and then relaxes to bask in the accomplishment. Another salesperson reaches a sales goal and becomes complacent and self-satisfied.

Or perhaps you have been aware of the sales slump that too often occurs after a successful sales contest. Can the total blame be the success of the contest itself? Or are the salespeople letting down their efforts for what they feel is a well-deserved rest? For whatever reason the salesperson has settled for less than his or her potential.

Your written communication with your salespeople can be a valuable tool for spurring success into even greater achievement. The letters we have included in this section have proven useful for this purpose. Most of them contain two common and essential elements:

1. *A reward.* The behavioral scientists have confirmed through research that we all work to satisfy certain needs. The salesperson will put forth the second effort if his job offers the possibility for satisfying any of these needs.

    a) The salesperson will put forth extra effort for recognition — a pat on the back. It is not just recognition from the boss that is sought, but also from other salespeople, from the spouse, from others in the organization and the community. Providing the recognition the salesperson seeks will spur her to greater production.

    b) The salesperson will work harder for a sense of accomplishment — a feeling that he is providing some worthwhile value to the company, to other employees, to the community, to his family. Although money the salesperson receives provides a portion of this sense of accomplishment (for what is money but a measure of the salesperson's value), the sales manager can supplement and emphasize the sense of accomplishment the job provides.

    c) The salesperson will exert extra effort for a sense of participation in the decisions which affect him or her. The salesperson wants to feel that the boss and the company value good suggestions. The sales person wants to have some influence on the decisions that affect him or her. The sales manager who seeks his salespeople's contributions can often motivate them to ever greater performance.

    d) Salespeople will strive with greater effort for the opportunity for growth and advancement. Younger salespeople need to become professional in their sales skills. Others are seeking an opportunity to prepare for management positions.

2. *A challenge.* This is the "carrot" that is held out suggesting even greater rewards for additional effort. Where the reward focuses on past performance, the challenge directs attention and effort on future opportunity. Many salespeople will motivate themselves by keeping a challenge or goal perpetually before them. Others constantly require the challenge to be laid

before them. In either situation, the astute sales manager can gain extra effort from his sales force with well-calculated and continuing challenges.

1. CONGRATULATIONS ON AN OUTSTANDING SALE

When a salesperson makes that extraordinary sale, it's an experience to be shared. Even though the salesperson receives a handsome commission for the effort, she or he seeks a reward that, to him or her, may be even more important — recognition. Provide recognition and you set the stage for further effort; ignore it and it could be the last extra effort the salesperson makes.

Notice that the model letter is specific about what the salesperson has accomplished. Not only does this help the sales rep to recognize exactly what it is that you are complimentary about, it lets him or her know you care enough to dig out the details.

Timing is important as it is in all motivational letters. Let the salesperson know you are aware of his or her accomplishment as soon as you learn about it. Also valuable: let others important to the salesperson know what has been accomplished — then tell him or her you have spread the word.

Model Letter 1-1

Dear _____:

It isn't a common occurence, so when it happens it's something to shout about!   **(a)**

I'm referring to your recent sale to Central Whole-sale Hardware. Not only is this dealer one of the largest in the division, it's one we have been trying unsuccessfully to land for a long time. And the fact that you accomplished this feat single-handedly from initial proposal to close, adds immeasurably to your credit.

So shout is what I've been doing. The Vice President   **(b)**
of Sales has heard all about what you have been able to do and so has the Product Manager.

Before you move on to even greater achievements let's take a moment to review just what you did to bring off this important sale. Perhaps you would like to take a few minutes at next Monday's sales meeting to tell everyone how you were able to bring it off.

Also, I have taken steps to have this letter placed in your personnel jacket. Anyone considering you for promotion will want to know about this important achievement.

Sincerely,

Alternate Wording:

(a) I just got word on your terrific achievement.

(a) I was just looking over your sales call report and was overjoyed to see your outstanding accomplishment.

(b) I'm like the proud dad that has to brag about his son's accomplishments. And am I bragging. V.P. Bill Johnson was the first to hear. He would like to have you tell him about it personally the first time you are in the office. Also, the account of your sale will be in next week's sales newsletter.

2. CONGRATULATIONS ON WINNING A SALES CONTEST

A sales contest by its very nature provides winners with desired recognition. However, you can get considerably more mileage from your contests by careful wording of your letter of congratulations. This model letter helps you realize extra benefits from a contest, not only by patting the sales representative on the back but by pointing the rep to even greater achievements.

Notice the conciseness of this letter makes it suitable for framing. It's difficult to frame a two-page letter.

Model Letter 1-2

Dear _____:

Congratulations on winning first place in the Region 76 "Plus 10" drive. Signing 15 new accounts during the 60-day contest is a remarkable achievement.

I'm sure you worked both smarter and harder in the past 60 days. The rewards you will enjoy as a result go far beyond the winning of the contest.

To highlight only one benefit — the feeling of a job well done must be in your mind. And it deserves to be.

Your wife, Barbara, must be proud of your accomplishment and her support must have been most important to you as you made those extra calls. **(a)**

When you and Barbara return from your award trip, we should discuss the sales techniques you found most helpful in winning the contest. We have a great opportunity this year and the thought you invested during this contest can continue to pay you big dividends in increased sales and commissions. **(b)**

Sincerely,

Alternate Wording:

(a) Your wife, Barbara, must be proud of your accomplishment and her support must have been most important to you as you made those extra calls. I have taken the opportunity to send her a note explaining what you have been able to accomplish and thanking her for her part in this remarkable achievement.

(a) I have taken the liberty to provide a press release to our local newspaper apprising them of your achievement.

(b) Enclosed is your first-place award check for $_____. You probably have already become aware that this extra money can be yours each and every month by continuing with the effort and techniques you have used during the contest. Your commissions for the new business you sold during the contest period nearly equals the award check. Is that a goal worth shooting for?

3. LETTERS TO THE SALES FORCE ANNOUNCING RESULTS OF A SALES CONTEST

A successful sales contest benefits more than the winners. In fact everyone on the sales force stands to gain as a result. The losers should gain the incentive to try harder. And everyone should benefit through understanding of what is required to sell the really tough prospects.

To gain maximum benefit from a sales contest, then, requires the sales manager to follow through after the contest. With the results of the contest, the manager can provide continuing incentive to the entire sales force and can encourage all his salespeople to use on a daily basis the techniques which caused the winners to perform so outstandingly.

Model Letter 1-3

Dear _____:

The contest results are in. Everybody is a winner. Well, that's not quite the case. But we did get some great sales performance during the contest. Those persons will get the prizes and the recognition. The enclosed sheet provides the official contest results.

Our congratulations to Sue Caldwell and to Dick Butke for an outstanding job. Bill Jones turned in a remarkable performance, too.

Now, more about everyone being a winner. Everyone may not get the recognition or the rewards of the top producers but they will surely get something as valuable in the long run. Some of you have learned what can be done with a well-thought-out sales plan and extra effort. Others have discovered some important new sales ideas that work. What you have been able to achieve during the contest can be continued every day. All it takes is following through with the same resolution, hard work, and smart selling that you used so well during the contest.

There is another bonus. I have asked the top producers to share with each of us the techniques that worked so well during the contest. During our next sales meeting they will be explaining what they did and how it can be duplicated in your own territory.

So you see each of you *is* a winner in this contest. All that's required to get the payoff is the diligent application of what you have learned in the past six weeks.

Sincerely,

4. FOR THE SALES REP'S PART IN HELPING THE SALES OFFICE WIN A SALES CONTEST

Most sales representatives respond positively when asked to contribute to a team effort. This is a need that springs from his desire for participation. The key to successful motivation through team effort is adequate and prompt follow-up recognition. Here is a letter that provides such recognition and, in addition, encourages the sales rep to even greater achievements.

Model Letter 1-4

Dear _____:

WE'RE NUMBER 1. And the $126,543 in business you wrote during the contest period made the difference.

As you know, Los Angeles was ahead of us during most of the contest. Only in the last week were we able to pull $23,000 ahead of them. If it were not for your extra effort (or for that matter the extra effort of any other member of this great sales team), it would have been a different story. But we can't let **(a)** down now. Los Angeles will be gunning for us. Let's not let them throw in our face that we won the contest, but only at the expense of future sales. *Keep the pressure on.*

From me and all the other sales representatives on the team, thanks for a job well done.

Sincerely,

Alternate Wording:

(a) As you may know, no division has been successful in keeping a position of number one for two consecutive quarters. I believe we're in a position to pull it off. How would it feel to be a member of a team who accomplishes something that's never been done before?

Here is a letter written by a sales manager whose sales force didn't quite win the contest but deserved a pat on the back anyway.

Model Letter 1-5

Dear _____:

Well, as it turns out we're number two. But that only means we will have to try harder. The Midwest Division beat us by just $62,000. That represents only about two sales from each of you.

But let me personally thank you for the extra effort that was so visible from you during this contest period. Your sales are up over $9,000 and it's easy to see from your sales call report just what has led to the sales increase — plenty of extra hard work and extra hours.

I personally believe we still deserve to be number one. As a matter of fact, I am so sure of it that I suggested to Midwest that we would beat them in total sales during the coming quarter. They're willing to take us on. An extra three sales per week could make the difference. How about it? Shall I tell them they have a bet?   **(a)**

Sincerely,

Alternate Wording:

(a) The sales bet we had with the Midwest Division cost us a little money and a lot of pride. It's not easy to take a back seat to Midwest.

5. SEEKING SUGGESTIONS FROM FIELD SALES REPRESENTATIVES

Suggestions and recommendations from the sales force are not only an important source of new ideas for improving the efficiency and sales of the organization, they are a means, if handled properly, for sales force motivation. When the sales manager solicits and accepts the idea of his salespeople, it is an indication he values their opinions. It tells the sales representatives they are needed and that they make an important contribution to the organization. The following letter taps this idea source and motivates the sales force to greater productivity.

Model Letter 1-6

Dear _____:

We all know that our new HY-POX industrial glove has some very desirable qualities. We also know it takes more than telling our customers about the tremendous advantages we have to offer.

Here's an opportunity to make an "above-the-call-of-duty" contribution to the company and your sales teammates. If you have found ways to demonstrate the unique qualities of the HY-POX line, let us know about them.

To be more specific, we need ways to demonstrate:

- The toughness of the HY-POX line;
- It s acid-resistant quality;
- The dexterity quality of the line;
- The wearing quality of the line.

Send your ideas to me. I'll make sure they are **(a)** circulated to the entire sales force. Besides providing a valuable service to the others in the organization, you will have the satisfaction of seeing your ideas grow and produce results.

Sincerely,

Alternate Wording:

(a) Dick Spencer has recently sent me an excellent idea for demonstrating HY-POX's acid-resistant quality. I'll be forwarding it to you in a few days. If you have ideas, send them along. I'll make sure they are distributed to the entire sales force.

(a) Just to make it interesting, here is a little contest. When all the ideas are published, we will ask each sales rep to vote on the most valuable demonstration idea. The sales reps who submit the three ideas judged most valuable by the sales force will each win $50.

Here is a letter that thanks the sales representative for his contribution and informs him that his idea will be used by the organization. Note the personal reference to the suggestion the sales representative has made.

Model Letter 1-7

Dear _____:

We are modifying the sales report as you suggested.

The addition of a results column and the use of a third copy for comparing results with plans will undoubtedly improve the planning and call efficiency of many sales reps. New forms are being printed and will be sent to the entire sales force next month.

Thanks for your idea, not only from me but from the other sales reps as well. Keep the ideas coming in. I value them as an "on the firing line" practical source.   **(a)**

Sincerely,

Alternate Wording:

(a) Remember, the more items you submit, the greater are your chances of winning one of the prizes for most valuable suggestion.

(a) As a special token of the sales department's appreciation for your idea, would you and Sue please accept dinner some evening at the restaurant of your choice. Just put the bill on your expense account.

Keep the ideas coming in. It's only through ideas such as yours that this company can maintain an edge over our competition.

The sales manager encounters a more difficult communication problem when the sales representative provides a suggestion that cannot be utilized by the organization. The manager must indicate that the idea is unacceptable but must do it in such a way that the sales rep continues to forward ideas. Note the letter's positive tone.

Model Letter 1-8

Dear _____:

Thanks for your suggestion concerning modification of our 260 Model Air Conditioner. It's through recommendations such as yours that we can be sure our air conditioner line is kept current with the needs of our customers. It's obvious that you have given considerable thought to your recommendation.

Your suggestion would probably have been accepted   **(a)**
if it had meshed with the long-range marketing plans for the product. The intention is to keep this line as a low-cost conditioner which appeals to a mass market. Your recommendation, although significant, would increase the cost of the conditioner beyond the competitive level.

The spirit with which you made your recommendation is commendable. Engineering and marketing need your suggestions. Keep them coming. Next time it may just be the most important contribution the company receives all year.

Sincerely,

Alternate Wording

(a) Engineering has considered your suggestion and feels that, although the benefits would be worthwhile, the technical complexity of the modification would subject the conditioner to frequent and costly repairs. For this reason they feel your suggestion must await the time when simpler methods of application are developed.

6. ENCOURAGING SUPPORT FROM A SPOUSE

The sales representative's spouse provides an important back-up source for encouragement and support. The successful salesperson must frequently take extra time away from his spouse and family. Sometimes that involves travel, working evenings, giving up vacations. The spouse who is indifferent to the salesperson's career or is unwilling to make the sacrifices that contribute to the successful career, can quickly destroy the best-conceived motivational program. Many sales managers continually work to keep the spouse informed and to show appreciation for the spouse's support. This letter fits this category.

Model Letter 1-9

Dear _____:

I can't tell you how much it meant to all the sales force who attended the National Sales Conference last week to have Kathy assist as one of the instructors in our seminar programs.

As you already know, Kathy has a tremendous amount of talent and experience and her willingness to share her knowledge with the newer people, as well as those who have been with the company for some time, was truly appreciated by everyone present.

I know it was an imposition on you and on Kathy to ask her to come in early since it meant she would be away from home a little longer, and, of course, we realize that some time was lost from her territory. However, I'm sure that the results will be a gain in the productiveness of the people she taught. Additionally, I'm sure that Kathy will find that she too has learned a great deal from the experience. It's true that the teacher learns as much or more than the student.

Thanks again for your understanding and your kind cooperation.

Sincerely,

Occasionally there comes a sales event that requires the participation of both the sales representative and spouse. Perhaps it is a dinner with a client, or a trade show which customer spouses will be attending. Such occasions can present a problem when the spouse is pursuing his or her own career. This letter seeks to justify the time that the spouse is being requested to take to share in the event.

Model Letter 1-10

Dear _____ :

As Randy joins the Acme sales team let me welcome you too as an official member. I recognize that you have your own career to pursue and it surely takes a good share of your time and concentration. But just as Randy will want to be supportive of you in certain events that your job requires, I am sure you will want to assist Randy when the occasion demands.

As with any sales career, there are times when emotional support is valuable from a spouse — a pat on the back for a tough sale; reassurance when things are not going well; encouragement to stay with it when persistence will pay off.

But I'm also talking about more direct assistance that may be required. It may require your participation in an evening out with a client. Or perhaps accompanying Randy to an out-of-town trade show on occasion. There can be nothing mandatory about such support activities, of course, and I wouldn't want them to be. But I encourage you to support

Randy with your presence at such events whenever possible.

The word that comes to mind here is "synergism": the sum is greater than the parts. You and your family will benefit from such assistance through greater sales and income as well as through the satisfaction that you have shared in a worthwhile endeavor.

I realize that you surely want to assist Randy to succeed in any manner possible and that you are aware of what I have mentioned here. My emphasis is added only to clarify and solidify resolve in the months and years to come. **(a)**

Welcome to the team.

Sincerely,

Alternate Wording:

(a) The first opportunity to provide your support in a formal way will occur soon. As Randy has probably told you, there will be a trade show in San Antonio during February in which Randy will be participating. Your support and presence at that show will provide Randy with contacts and friendships not open to him otherwise. If you can attend your mutual effort will be "synergistic."

7. FOR REACHING A GOAL

Sales and personal goals can be a highly motivating force — but only if the sales manager makes reaching them important. This letter was written to recognize the outstanding efforts of the sales representative to reach a goal and to encourage the rep to continue striving to meet new goals.

Model Letter 1-11

Dear _____:

When you and I sat down to work out your goal plan for the year, I believe we agreed that your's was an ambitious goal that would require a great amount of extra effort and smart selling. I also said that I believed you had what it would take to meet your goal.

It's nice to be proven correct. Congratulations on meeting your sales goals right down the line. What you have been able to accomplish called for innovative selling, persistence, and a willingness to sacrifice.

Enclosed is your bonus check that you have earned as **(a)** a result of meeting your goals.

Today's accomplishments, as great as they are, **(b)** become tomorrow's base from which to work. I know from my previous experience with you that you will want to move on from here to greater accomplishments. Let's plan on meeting next Monday morning to establish your next year's goals.

Sincerely

Alternate Wording:

(a) Enclosed is your bonus check that you have earned as a result of meeting your goals. In addition, Mr. Harris has requested that we have a small get-together dinner for all the sales reps and their spouses who, such as you, have been so successful in the past year. I will be letting you know shortly about the details of that dinner.

(b) Now, since this an "I love you greatly, but what have you done for me lately" organization, I know you will want to be thinking what you intend to accomplish during the coming year. Now's the time to take a fresh assessment of your assets and your needs to determine what you can reasonably expect to achieve in the coming plan period. I'll be setting a date with you during the next week.

2

MODEL LETTERS THAT MOTIVATE SALESPEOPLE TO ACT ON YOUR SUGGESTIONS

2

MODEL LETTERS THAT MOTIVATE SALESPEOPLE TO ACT ON YOUR SUGGESTIONS

Nothing in life is certain except change. Yet we resist change. Our salespeople don't want to change. But a large part of our job as sales managers is to get our salespeople to change. We want them to try new methods, use new sales aids, follow up on new advertising and promotion campaigns, sell new products, call on new industries, market segments, and prospects.

We could just order them to do it our way. Sometimes we do. Sometimes that works. And sometimes it doesn't.

We know that if each salesperson believes in the new approach and adopts it as his or her own, they will take it and run with it — produce results. So we must sell them on how they will gain from change. Selling is what we do, our specialty. Selling the sales force on doing it our way should be easy.

However, we grew up on face-to-face selling, eyeball-to-eyeball communication. If our sales force is spread out over a large territory, this may complicate our communication. We will make calls in the territory with the salespeople and we will have them in to our office, both individually and as a group from time to time. As a practical matter, timeliness will often dictate that we rely on phone and letter to get our ideas and suggestions put into action immediately until we can follow up with face-to-face communication. We recognize that eye-to-eye is always the most desirable mode of persuasive communication. If the information to be communicated is at the very core of the sales force-company relationship, such as a change in the commission and base pay arrangement or a change in ownership of the company, we would call the sales force together in meetings to guarantee the highest possible quality two-way communication. More often, however, what we want is for the sales force to follow up on a mailing being done in their territory by the sales promotion people at the home office, or to use a new sales aid or a/v device provided by headquarters or a supplier. It may not be worth spending $500 or $5,000 to bring the sales force together, much less the even higher cost of two or three lost selling days.

There remains the telephone or the letter. The telephone is a powerful tool because it is immediate, personal, and informal. But it is fleeting, temporary, providing the listener no means of reviewing the most important points after the call — unless we were so persuasive they took complete notes. Research has taught us that when we rely on the ear alone as a message receiver, no more than 30% of the communication is likely to be retained. When the eye can be included as a receiver, retention can be expected to jump to as much as 80% or more. Direct mail and telecommunication experts agree that mail and phone combined can provide more than double the response from prospects than either method used alone. The message is clear — the letter has a definite place in getting ideas across to our sales force, changing behavior to what we want, and increasing sales.

Getting your ideas and suggestions put into action by means of a letter is not much different from the personal sales job you do when convincing your people in person to use an idea. The following model letters generally rely on a four-step approach to convince the reader to take action on the manager's idea:

1. Secure the reader's interest in what you want to suggest. To accomplish this, appeal to the selfish interest of the reader.

2. Identify and discuss the problem standing in the way of sales and commissions which led you to write this letter to the salesperson.

3. Develop a solution to the problem with a description of personal benefits which the salesperson will receive.

4. Ask for action by the salesperson. Ask him or her to use the idea/method/tool and report results.

1. ENCOURAGING THE SALES REPRESENTATIVE TO SELL AN UNTAPPED MARKET

When you find a new application for your product or service, or market research uncovers an emerging market segment — a whole new group of prospects, you want your sales force making effective sales calls on them as quickly as possible. A letter will probably be the most efficient method for informing your sales force. If hard-to-understand concepts are involved, a series of one-on-one coaching calls with your salespeople will follow shortly. Often, however, all that is needed is understanding of the sales opportunity and specific steps to follow and the sales force will enthusiastically call on the previously untapped market.

Model Letter 2-1

Dear _____:

If you suddenly became aware of $1,000,000 in new **(a)** business in your territory what would you do about it? Did you say "I'll start calling on these new prospects today — I can sell one-fourth of them by accident and another one-fourth with my magnetic sales personality — that's $500,000, before I even begin to use my amazing professional selling skill"?

Well, we've become aware of a new potential market. What would it take to convince you to go after it?

- Proof that you could tap it?
- A tested method for selling it?
- The sales tools to make a professional presentation?

As a company, we have neglected the car dealer market. They were experiencing some tough going for a while and were hard to call on and we didn't see the strong potential for our product. But the auto business is going strong now and our market research has shown our products fit this market. There are over 50 new automobile dealers in your territory. One of them is a customer. According to our market research the average dealership purchases over $20,000 in oil products annually. Sell five of them and you add $100,000 in volume and that's only 10% of the potential. Can you do it? We believe you can. We tried a market test in four sales territories and used the experience to develop a sales approach to this prospect group. Over a four-month trial period, the salespeople generated $350,000 additional sales (projected into annual figures) in this lucrative new market.

How did they do it? With this sample plan:

1. Identify prospects. I'm enclosing a list of dealers in your territory. Sales volume is indicated and I suggest you concentrate on the largest.

2. Develop your own style for presenting our program. A visual/flip chart was developed during the test project and one is in the mail to you. When you get it you might want to talk to that dealer you are now selling and determine the biggest benefits of our new program from his point of view.

3. Start making appointments. During the market test 62% of those contacted agreed to an appointment when the opener/interest-getter used was offering our credit card as a means of extending credit to the dealer's customers at nominal cost to the dealership.

4. Make your presentation. See description below of sales tools provided.

5. Make a formal proposal. We'll help. Just provide us with name, address, expected volume, key interest areas, and we will send a

formal proposal to the individual you specify and send a copy to you.

6. Follow up to get action. Make a follow-up call within ten working days.

The following sales tools are in the mail to you to help insure success.

- A visual/flip chart presentation-feature/-advantage/benefit of our new car dealer program.

- A detailed brochure describing our credit card program for dealers.

- A product brochure of lubricants for auto dealership applications.

- Car dealer testimonials you can use in your sales calls.

Immediately, send me your goal for: **(b)**

1. How many car dealers you expect to sell each quarter of the next 12 months.

2. How many formal presentations you expect to make to car dealers for each quarter over the next 12 months.

3. How many car dealers you expect to call for an appointment for each quarter of the next 12 months.

I will be expecting your goals by May 15.

Sincerely,

Alternate Wording:

(a) How would you like to earn an extra $1,500 bonus this year? Our Market research department just proved that it is possible with a market test in several territories similar to yours. How was it done?

(b) Please call me on Wednesday, May 15, so we can discuss this plan. Be prepared to ask any questions that will help your understanding and be prepared to tell me how you plan to implement the program.

Model Letter 2-2

Dear _____:

It seems we spend our whole life in a constant search   **(a)**
for new clients. Our current customers are fully
invested, move, die, or even become infatuated with
some new approach a competitor brings them.

Do you sometimes, in a weak moment, believe you
have contacted every doctor, lawyer, accountant,
business owner, and big company officer in town?
What if you discovered a whole new category of
prospect? What if we could reach out and touch them
for you by direct mail? If this happened would you
reach out to them with a timely phone call, and would
you continue to follow up when you discover an area
of interest and need you can satisfy through your
professional market expertise and our complete line
of financial products and services?

We have found a whole new market segment which
meets most of our criteria for highly qualified prospective clients. Much has been written recently
about the proliferation of consultants and consulting
organizations in computer software and related
fields of design and engineering. We have obtained a
list of these new successful entrepreneurs. In a small
test project, a group of investment counselors had
approximately 40% higher requests for further information from this group than with their own new
prospect list.

Of those who requested information, an exceptional
number became investors. Please phone me at 3:30
p.m. next Monday to discuss coordinating a mailing
and follow-up. I'm sure you'll be as enthusiastic as I
am with the potential in this prospective client group.

Sincerely,

Alternate Wording:

(a) Do you ever have enough new prospects? No matter how
content and prosperous your customers are, normal attrition
makes new prospects a necessity. Our current customers are

fully invested, move, die, or even become infatuated with some new approach a competitor brings them.

2. INFORMING THE SALES FORCE ABOUT ANOTHER SALESPERSON'S SUCCESSFUL METHODS

How do you get one salesperson to accept and begin using methods and techniques that are producing superior results for another? The difficulty in getting such new ideas accepted lies with the defense mechanism in each salesperson's mind when they are asked to adopt the ideas of a peer. It's a natural part of the sales job to feel a need to be creative. But even Einstein said he only had one truly original idea in his entire working life. There is a lot to be said for utilizing proven methods. Here is a letter to sell the troops on using the methods of their friendly competitors.

Model Letter 2-3

Dear _____:

Time is money. That's almost a cliché but just last **(a)** week a friend of yours proved it's still true.

Brian Watts has made a practice of checking with the prospect's banker sometime after making his first call and before making a presentation. Brian admits it takes time to accomplish this. He has had to work with the bankers in his territory to get them to cooperate. But after that it takes only a telephone call to determine if the prospect has the financial capacity to buy.

Brian reports that just last week he made a check with a banker on a prospect only to discover the prospect is in deep financial trouble. Had he failed to make this check, it would have cost him an estimated ten to twelve hours of sales time only to learn that the prospect couldn't buy. Now he's more sold than ever on the wisdom of checking first with the banker.

There's another advantage to qualifying the prospect by first checking with the banker. You can often develop some additional helpful information about the prospect that will assist you in selling him.

Can you line up the cooperation of just two bankers   **(b)**
in your territory as a starter? Some time invested in
this direction now can mean many more profitable
hours of actual selling time later.

Would you send me your thoughts about this
qualifying method when you send your weekly plan
and expense reports next Friday. Please include the
names of the banks you're going to start with.

Sincerely,

Alternate Wording:

(a) Think back over your prospect list for the past month. How
     many prospects have you thought you had sold only to find
     they couldn't finance their purchase?

     Brian Watts did that just a few months ago and found that he
     was losing valuable time for profitable selling by trying to sell
     the prospect who didn't have the financial capacity to buy. As a
     result he has made a practice of checking with the prospect's
     banker sometime after making the first call and before making
     a presentation.

(b) I would like to have your ideas on how you would put a
     program like this into operation in your own area. Think it
     through and let me have the results sometime in the next
     week.

3. CONVINCING THE SALES FORCE TO USE A NEW SALES AID

The sales force doesn't always grab the latest sales tool provided
them by headquarters or the sales manager and run to try it out on the
closest prospect. Sometimes they think the sales aid will be more trouble
to use than it's worth. Sometimes they haven't been convinced that the
new sales tool will dramatize a sales point strongly enough to convince a
prospect. They may be afraid they'll lose the prospect's attention and
interest during the time it takes to set up the sales aid. Why is that? Well,
they may have received a sales tool sometime in their past selling life
which the sales promotion people worked out with much creativity and
thought, but didn't take out into a territory and try themselves to see how
it worked with real prospects. And maybe it was more trouble than it was
worth, and maybe it actually got in the way of the sale. They may have
been "helped" by a mailing in the past which turned out to be sent to a list

which contained practically no qualified prospects for their product, and they made 40 calls before finding one qualified prospect, and they can average one out of ten making straight cold calls.

Salespeople can have valid reasons for being skeptical of new sales aids and support we offer them. If we have a new sales tool or sales support device we know will increase their productivity, it's worth our extra effort to make sure the troops enthusiastically use the new tool.

Model Letter 2-4

Dear _____:

When you are with a skeptical prospect and you know our quality is important to them, have you ever wished you could transport that prospect into our plant *right now* and let them see our care and quality control for themselves? Did you ever wish you could have one of your satisfied customers standing next to you to tell your prospect how consistent our quality is and how dependable we are?

Well, now you can have a tour of the factory at your   **(a)** fingertips and satisfied customers at your side on every call, and our service crews and a detailed explanation of our creative financing availability as well.

You will receive a videocassette within a couple of days which will provide you all of these advantages and more in a sales situation. The sales promotion department has completed a videotape combining a plant tour, satisfied customer testimonials, and a clear, simple presentation of our financing. The entire tape is nine minutes and should hold the interest of your toughest prospect. Salespeople and sales managers were involved throughout the production. Several salespeople have been using it on a test basis for two months, and the original tape was revised with some minor changes based on prospect reactions during the test.

The salespeople who cooperated in the test are   **(b)** enthusiastic about the effect the tape has on prospects. Personally, I'm eager to come out and make calls with you and see the results for myself. You know Charley Short, my fellow regional manager in Chicago — he was in the field test with his salespeople, and he raves about it.

I'll phone Friday about 4:30 p.m. and we'll discuss the tape. I'm sure you'll have received it and viewed it several times by then.

Sincerely,

Alternate Wording:

(a) Salespeople across the country have been working with the sales promotion manager for several months and have produced a videotape which does just that.

(b) You've heard me talk about Charley Short, who started out in sales with me and is now regional manager in Chicago. He and several of his people were involved in making this tape — so I know it's good.

Model Letter 2-5

Dear _____:

How often have you waited for engineering to get   **(a)** back to you with capacity estimates in the past year? Or worried about losing the prospect's interest, or a competitor coming in before you could get back with the information? Would you like to be able to provide estimates accurate to +/–5% on the spot?

I've been working with engineering and we've come up with two tools which will enable you to provide capacity estimates on the spot 90% of the time. For short-distance, smaller jobs we've developed a slide rule type device. Just select the category of material handled, distance, number of turns/bends, and degree of bend and you will have the capacity per hour. For larger jobs, engineering has put together a computer program that will enable you to call in the same variables and they'll have estimated capacity for you in minutes. These capacities will have to be represented to the prospect as a ballpark estimate, and our field engineer will come on site to do accurate measurements and determine all variables accurately. We'll have a meeting a week from Monday so engineering can instruct us in the use of both of these tools and answer questions. We'll also practice working with both tools with some typical installations.

I'm sure you share my enthusiasm for this new approach which will provide quick response and a professional approach. I'll see you a week from Monday when we really become familiar with these new sales tools.

Sincerely,

Alternate Wording:

(a) How would you like to be able to provide prospects with on-the-spot capacity estimates? No more having to say "I'll get back to you when engineering provides me the figures" — then worrying for a week that your prospect is talking to our competitor.

4. FOCUSING THE SALES FORCE ON A PARTICULAR PRODUCT

There are times when every sales manager must direct the efforts of the sales force toward a particular product. Perhaps the salespeople are neglecting a high profit line. Or inventories may be out of line requiring concentrated sales effort to recover working capital. These are situations for which a sales force letter is particularly well-suited.

Model Letter 2-6

Dear _____:

HELP! Your special effort is needed. The company is **(a)** swamped by oversized inventories in our 360 and 660 models. Sluggish sales in these lines during the past six months have swollen our inventory. To assist you in moving the excess fast, you are authorized to offer 22% off normal dealer price until June 30. All orders must be shipped by the June 30th date to qualify.

Here's where you personally benefit. For every unit you sell in either the 360 or 660 line between now and June 30, you earn an extra $5. Now's your chance to earn several hundred dollars in extra commission.

Here's how:

1. Begin today to check dealer stock for adequate inventory.
2. Get POP displays out front where they sell.
3. Sell for inventory. Dealers can make big profits by stocking ahead.
4. Talk the 360 and 660 line to everyone you call on. I will be checking weekly with you on this important sales effort. We must reduce inventory Now.

Sincerely,

Alternate Wording:

(a) Looking for some extra cash? Here's a fast way to get it and at the same time be of service to your dealers.

Sluggish sales in our 360 and 660 models have pushed up inventories. To work them off we are authorized to offer a 22%-off-dealer-list discount until June 30.

Here is a letter written to place special emphasis on increasing sales of the highest profit item in the product line.

Model Letter 2-7

Dear _____:

You are aware of the trend toward lower profit **(a)** margins throughout our industry. Holding the margin is important to all of us. That profit is what pays for the advertising and promotion programs that give us a little selling edge over the competition and keeps our commission and bonus setup the best in the industry. Profit margin is important to you, me, and the company.

You know our premium line is where the profit is. In your own territory, the premium line accounts for 30% of your sales and over 45% of the gross profit generated. An extra 10% in sales in this line would increase profit 21%.

In the day-to-day fight to get the order — any order — and faced with price competition, the natural tendency is to start with the middle of the line and drop to the discount stuff if a competitor comes in lower. I believe quality still sells and I know you do, too. Sell is the key word. It's easy to fall into the trap of order-taking and just bringing out lower-priced goods. There is room for an increase in sales in the premium line in your territory. Your premium line sales are 6% lower than the company national average. I'm sure you will agree that your territory has more than an average number of quality stores.

I believe a 10% increase in premium line sales is **(b)** realistic in your territory without any loss in number of orders. In other words, I believe you can still walk in and sell quality from the start if you concentrate on it. I've calculated the effect of this strategy on your total volume for the year, by the way, and I'm quite sure you would be in a position for Sales Person of the Year with this increase.

Think about it. Get out your customer list and see how you feel about 10% more premium as a realistic goal. Then call me Friday and let's discuss specifically where the increase comes from.

Sincerely,

Alternate Wording:

(a) Profit is the name of the game. And of course the premium line is where our highest profit is.

(b) A 21% profit increase would put you among the top three most profitable territories in the Division. And territory profitability is one of the factors considered in management placement considerations.

5. AIMING SALESPEOPLE AT TARGET ACCOUNTS

If, to adapt an old saying, your salesperson can't see the tree for the forest, you may need this type of letter to call attention to an important prospect opportunity.

Model Letter 2-8

Dear _____:

The climate may be just about right for you to make a call on:

> Acme Tool and Grinding
> 132 East Front Street
> Middletown, ...
> Steel Purchasing contact: John Garcia

As you may be aware, this prospect is a customer of Bryson, Inc. We have an indication that they are having difficulty getting delivery on tool steel. So now might be the perfect time to make an appointment. I will be watching your call reports for the results.

Sincerely,

6. FOLLOW UP AND REINFORCE COACHING CALLS WITH SALESPEOPLE

Letters can be a valuable aid in getting individuals to put into action suggestions you made during personal coaching sessions. Verbal communication is fragile and temporary. Even if your suggestion was important to the salesperson at the time, it can become hazy, unclear, or be forgotten when you're gone. A follow-up letter draws attention to a particular discussion area and puts in writing the main points discussed.

Model Letter 2-9

Dear _____:

I enjoyed the two days we spent making calls last week. That character managing the fuel company in Merril will bring a smile to my face whenever I think about first calls for a long time to come. Refreshing people and situations like that are part of what makes sales such an exciting and enjoyable career — there's always something new and different. That particular call did lead us into a subject that is important if you are going to reach your goal in new accounts this year. We agreed it's important to minimize surprises   **(a)** on the first call. We reviewed some of the sources of prospecting and qualifying information available to you (list attached). Also, we agreed you need those cross-reference directories you found were available from a local directory publisher in Madison. Have them send the bill to me.

We also agreed upon a step-by-step pre-call preparation that will enable you to know what individual you need to see, to have a benefit offer opener ready, and to have some questions ready to use. You will have a strategy for nailing down a 30- to 60-minute business discussion meeting. Call me Monday and we'll discuss how these methods are working. Also, **(b)** let's agree upon a convenient time in June for us to spend another couple of days on calls checking our progress on this approach for increasing new accounts.

Sincerely,

Alternate Wording:

(a) We agreed you've got to strengthen your approach on first calls. In order to do that you need to devote more care to prospecting and qualifying.

(b) I'll call you next Monday and you can outline your plan for increasing the ratio of appointments per first call on prospects. And I'll have some June dates set to come back and ride with you and check progress on this project.

Model Letter 2-10

Dear _____:

Tuesday and Wednesday were interesting and profitable days. Not only did you make some important sales, but you gave me some excellent ideas to pass on to the sales force. I hope you got some new ideas as well.

Wednesday afternoon we talked about the need to develop a clear-cut list of benefits your prospect could expect to receive as a result of buying your product. The prospect is interested in the features of your product only to the extent that he/she believes the feature satisfies some need. Don't assume the prospect sees a clear connection between the features of your product and some personal need. That can lose a sale. Be careful to clearly describe each end result/benefit in personal terms related to the prospect's situation.

The result of this close tailoring to prospects needs will be increased sales. I'm sure this will be of great value to you as you develop your territory.

Work on this area for the next week and when we get together again on the 18th, we'll discuss how you have progressed. I know you will find that your prospect's interest and desire will sharpen considerably. **(a)**

Thanks again for a very worthwhile two days last week.

Sincerely,

Alternate Wording:

(a) Just to sharpen your skill in translating features to customer benefits when you are planning each sales call for the coming week, take each feature of the product you intend to discuss and write out the benefits you think will be important to the prospect. Hold on to your list and we will discuss it when we are together on the 18th.

3

EFFECTIVE LETTERS TO ATTRACT TOP SALES PRODUCERS TO YOUR ORGANIZATION

3

EFFECTIVE LETTERS TO ATTRACT TOP SALES PRODUCERS TO YOUR ORGANIZATION

A large part of the sales management function is building and maintaining a strong, capable group of salespeople providing full coverage of the territory entrusted to us. Promotion, transfer, failure to produce, retirement, leaving for another opportunity — all of these factors are threats to our fully staffed sales force. And one empty territory out of ten means volume is only 90% of what it should be. So we are always recruiting and selecting salespeople. Much of our activity in the selection process is verbal; interviews with candidates, reference checks with previous employers. But most of our recruiting activity consists of written communication. Ads must be placed in various newspapers. Agencies must be contacted. Replies from candidates must be acknowledged. Additional information may be requested beyond that initially supplied by the applicant. Requests for interviews must be extended. Offers of employment must be made.

Candidates will be influenced by the letters you write. Stuffy, overly formal letters signal job applicants to beware of an organization that may stifle initiative and creativity. Lively, professional letters attract professional salespeople who may become your top producers. When you must turn away an unqualified applicant, you must do it in a way that preserves good will. This candidate may not meet our criteria right now, but a year or two from now he/she may be just what you need in your sales force. And you never know if they will become an influential executive at one of your major accounts.

1. SOLICITING SALES CANDIDATE LEADS

Really outstanding salespeople are worth searching for. That calls for effort beyond running newspaper ads. Some companies constantly communicate with other companies, employees, and customers searching for sales professionals. The following letter is used periodically even though no opening may exist at that moment. Experience has taught this company that openings occur frequently enough to be constantly searching for qualified people.

Model Letter 3-1

Dear _____:

In three minutes you can do someone a big favor and it won't cost you a dime!

You may know capable, mature people who are qualified and should seriously consider the insurance industry for a profitable, fulfilling career. We are looking for such men and women for positions in sales and sales management.

With our ever-expanding base of insurance and **(a)** financial investment programs and our marketing depth, unique opportunities are present for persons with successful experience or interest in insurance or other sales fields. Just write the names of people you **(b)** think might like to receive a free copy of an informative pamphlet entitled "Selecting Your Life Work."

Please do it now. Your friends and I will appreciate it.

Sincerely,

Alternate Wording:

(a) We have a unique opportunity for the right person. The individual we seek has at least three years of successful sales experience in industrial equipment. He/she is a college graduate, is currently employed, and is ambitiously watching for a better opportunity.

(b) If such an individual comes to mind, just jot his/her name and address or telephone number at the bottom of this letter, and return it to me in the enclosed self-addressed envelope.

Letter Indicating Interest in a Recommended Salesperson Who Has Not Applied for Employment

Occasionally you hear about an extraordinary salesperson employed elsewhere who is worth going after. Perhaps it is the result of the letter suggested above. Or perhaps a customer or acquaintance has volunteered a prospect. These letters are used as an initial approach to the highly recommended salesperson.

Model Letter 3-2

Dear _____:

We have never met, but a mutual acquaintance has **(a)** told me something of your sales ability and accomplishments.

Your background and approach sound similar to some of our most successful people. I believe you might find our product, backup services, and earning potential most interesting.

Please phone me in the next week if you are interested in meeting.

I believe we would have a mutually enjoyable discussion of capital goods sales at the very least.

Sincerely,

Alternate Wording:

(a) Sam Fowler, a long-time friend of mine whose opinion I respect, has told me something of your sales ability and accomplishments.

Model Letter 3-3

Dear _____ :

Your name has been referred to us most favorably. **(a)** We have no way of knowing whether this will be of interest to you or if you are perfectly satisfied in your present situation.

We have an opening in sales which can be very lucrative for the right person. If you would like to explore your possibilities in this growth industry, please call me at _____. If I am not in, leave **(b)** your phone number with my secretary along with the most convenient time to reach you.

Sincerely,

Alternate Wording:

(a) Your name has been referred to us most favorably by _____. (Better get permission of the referral source, but the use of the name will strengthen your approach.)

(b) We have a sales opening that may offer you new opportunity for growth, increased earnings, and work satisfaction.

Letter Acknowledging Receipt of Resumé and Indicating Interest

When you are in the midst of an all-out recruiting campaign to fill one or more sales positions, you will sometimes receive many responses in a short period of time. It may be physically impossible to personally contact each respondent immediately. But you don't want to lose the interest of any of the respondents — you don't know which one of them might be potentially your top producer next year. You should respond to all applicants immediately, indicating an interest in them and providing information to maintain their interest in your openings, while you organize all of the information you have received and prepare for interviews.

Model Letter 3-4

Dear _____ :

Thank you for expressing interest in the account executive position at _____ Company. We are pleased that you have taken the effort to explore this opportunity.

Our initial review of your resumé indicates that your background meets the major criteria established for this position. We received many responses, and therefore scheduling of interviews will take a bit longer. This position is important to our company and we will devote as much time as necessary to selecting the salesperson best qualified to serve our customers and maximize sales.

I've enclosed our annual report and product literature to further familiarize you with this opportunity. We will be in contact with you to schedule the next step within two weeks.

Sincerely,

Model Letter 3-5

Dear _____ :

Thank you for responding to our recent employment advertisement for the position of Sales Representative. Your background and experience are impressive, and you have many of the qualities we are seeking in applicants. We have received many applications and are proceeding as quickly as possible with the selection process. Be assured that we consider you a qualified candidate for this position. We will contact you as soon as possible to schedule an interview, certainly before the end of this month. Again, thank you for your expression of interest in our company.

Sincerely,

Model Letter 3-6

Dear _____:

Thank you for your resumé. It looks as if you have some important qualifications and experience that might fit the requirements for the position we have open.

I have enclosed a brochure describing our company   **(a)**
and products. I hope this material provides you additional insight into the background and nature of our business.

I will be in Chicago next week for interviews and look forward to meeting with you. I will phone you later this week to set up an appointment.

Sincerely,

Alternate Wording:

(a) I have attached our annual report which describes our company and products.

A Letter in Response to a Blind Inquiry

You may occasionally receive resumés and inquiries about sales openings from individuals who have not heard of a specific sales opening. These unsolicited, over-the-transom applicants may turn out to be totally unqualified and simply desperate and hungry. Then again, one of them may have the potential to break every company sales record. It's worth a little effort to keep their good will and interest in case an opening occurs unexpectedly in the near future.

Model Letter 3-7

Dear _____:

Thank you for your recent letter and information concerning your background and experience.

I'm sorry to say we do not have a position available presently that would meet your requirements or experience.

If we have an opening in the next few months and it   **(a)**
appears your qualifications match our requirements, I will contact you.

Thank you for thinking of our company in your search for new opportunity.

Sincerely,

Alternate Wording:

(a) I think it would be mutually beneficial to meet and further discuss our company and your background. Although we have no immediate opening, one never knows what may occur in the next few months.

Let's get to know each other in case an opportunity occurs in the near future. (To be used when the unsolicited applicant appears to be well-qualified.)

Requesting Additional Information from Sales Candidates

Sometimes you will receive a response from an applicant which does not provide as much initial information as you would like. It may be in the best interest of both the candidate and the sales manager to get that basic background information before investing the time and expense of telephone and/or face-to-face interviews.

Model Letter 3-8

Dear _____:

Thank you for your interest in our sales position opening. As our next step, we request that you complete the enclosed application and return it to us at your earliest convenience. Please complete the application in its entirety. Information concerning our company is attached.

When we have reviewed your application we will contact you.

Thank you for your interest in our organization. We look forward to hearing from you in the near future.

Sincerely,

Indicating the Desire for an Interview with a Sales Candidate

After initial screening of resumés and background information you will have a pool of candidates who look like they qualify. It's time to get face-to-face and see what they're really like. This letter explains what will be involved in the interview and helps the candidate to be prepared for the interview.

Model Letter 3-9

Dear _____ :

Thank you for responding to our ad in the *Tribune*.   **(a)**
Your resumé is interesting. I would like to discuss your experience in our industry further with you to see if this experience and your abilities could be successfully applied to our sales position.

I would like to meet with you at my office either next Wednesday or Thursday at 4:00 p.m. and we should be finished by 5:30 p.m. Please phone my secretary at _____ to confirm one of these dates or work out an alternative time with her if these won't work for you.

I look forward to meeting with you.

Sincerely,

Alternate Wording:

(a) Your resumé is interesting. We would like to discuss with you in more detail how your qualifications might match the needs of our position.

Declining Employment to a Prospective Salesperson Without an Interview

When you advertise to attract quality applicants for a sales opening, you may decide to run a "blind" ad, not identifying your company because you don't want competitors to know about your activity or to avoid the need to respond to every applicant, no matter how obviously unqualified they are.

On the other hand, you may believe that the prestige of your company will substantially increase the quantity and quality of response. When you give the company name, address, and even a name to write to, you may do much better than with a "blind box" ad according to some personnel experts. If you identify your company in the ad, common sense and PR (public relations) sense indicates a response is necessary to every applicant. In screening resumés and application forms, you will find some that simply do not meet standards of the job in terms of experience or education. Respond promptly to all applicants even though they fail to meet your minimum requirements. Permitting them to wonder what happened to their application is bad public relations. Your letter to these applicants should tell them definitely that they are no longer being considered for that position, but in a way that will not alienate them or insult them. After all, they may gain the necessary qualifications and reapply in the future. And they may be potential buyers of your products or services.

Model Letter 3-10

Dear _____:

Thank you for your interest in career opportunities with _____, Inc. We have reviewed your qualifications and work experience.

You have an excellent background, but your quali- **(a)** fications do not meet the exact specifications of our opening.

We appreciate your interest in our organization. We **(b)** will keep your resumé on file for future reference.

Sincerely,

Alternate Wording:

(a) Your work experience and education are impressive but do not exactly match our current opening.

(b) Your resumé will be kept on file, for we are a dynamic, expanding organization and anticipate future opportunities for people with your qualifications.

Model Letter 3-11

Dear _____:

Thank you for responding to our recent employment advertisement. Your background and experience are certainly impressive, and you have many of the qualities we are seeking in applicants.

I have found, however, that I have several other **(a)** applicants whose qualifications more closely match the requirements of this opening. With your permission I will keep your application on file, on the possibility that another opening might occur. Should something develop in the future which would be mutually beneficial, I will contact you.

Again, thank you for your interest in our company.

Sincerely,

Alternate Wording:

(a) Your resumé will be kept on file for the next six months. We will continue to match your background against similar job openings as they occur during that time. If you should desire to be considered after the six-month period, you should resubmit an updated resumé at that time.

Model Letter 3-12

Dear _____:

We have recently completed a selective screening of all resumés received in response to our advertisement for a National Account Executive. The candidates selected for preliminary interview have backgrounds closely corresponding to the position profile as we currently see the requirements. Your qualifications, experience, and career accomplishments distinguish you as an individual with potential for advancement in your field. We wish that circumstances would permit us to personally interview each candidate, but due to the large number of responses, that is not possible. We will keep your resumé on file for future consideration should a similar opening occur. Thank you for your interest.

Sincerely,

Declining Employment to a Prospective Salesperson After an Interview

Intensive recruiting should develop more prospects than you have openings. These additional prospects can provide a pool that may be tapped as future openings occur. Since applicants tend to reach for the next rung on the ladder, you will undoubtedly occasionally interview candidates who are close to your specifications but need just a little more experience. They may be just what you need a year from now.

The letter you send the refused applicant must be carefully worded in order to preserve good will and keep the door open for the future.

Model Letter 3-13

Dear _____:

I enjoyed our meeting October 12. Your approach to the marketplace is much like mine and I enjoyed sharing ideas.

I have reached a decision about our Territory Manager position. My final decision was based on the amount of experience the candidate had in our industry in a very similar market. I believe the person I hired has a chance to be one of our top producers due to the head start of identical experience.

I want to emphasize that you were one of the three finalists out of 300 applicants. That means that I have the highest regard for your ability. I will certainly contact you immediately should another opportunity open up. Thank you again for the time and effort you spent in the selection process. I am sure you will enjoy great success in any enterprise you undertake.

Sincerely,

Model Letter 3-14

Dear _____:

I enjoyed meeting with you last week.

We received over 100 applications, and you should be pleased to know that you were one of our final candidates. Unfortunately, we had only one opening **(a)** and only one person could get the job.

I want to thank you sincerely for the time and effort you invested in exploring career possibilities with our company. I am going to keep your resume in the front of my file and hope that the growth of our company will provide another opportunity for us to work together. I am sure that your talent and ambition will lead you to an interesting, challenging, and rewarding future.

Thanks again for your interest in our company.

Sincerely,

Alternate Wording:

(a) I want to emphasize that the person we hired had the advantage of a background which fit our opening perfectly. I only wish we had another position to offer you.

2. OFFERING EMPLOYMENT TO A CANDIDATE

Ideally, your offer of employment will be face-to-face. If a national position or transfer is involved, time and distance constraints may dictate extending an offer by telephone. Written communication will always be involved both as conventional formal follow-up and as a practical matter of clarifying in writing the terms of the employment agreement. And above all, your letter should remind your new salesperson of the advantages of joining your organization and encourage them to make (or stand by) a positive decision.

Model Letter 3-15

Dear _____:

I know you will be pleased to learn that in our estimation your experience, background, and knowledge puts you in a position to be highly successful in the job opportunity we discussed recently. We invite you to join our company as a sales representative.

As we discussed, when you have accepted this offer you will have the opportunity to complete our unique training program in Chicago. After nine weeks, you will be assigned to your territory.

As we discussed, your salary while in training will be $_____. When you are assigned, your salary will be $_____ and you will earn a commission of _____%.

You have impressed us with your talent and successful experience. I hope you will accept this offer which will be held open until May 29. When you decide to accept, call me collect and we will work out the details.

Congratulations, and I will look forward to your phone call.

Sincerely,

3. CLOSING CORRESPONDENCE WITH A SALES CANDIDATE WHO HAS DECLINED YOUR OFFER OF EMPLOYMENT

Unfortunately not every employment offer you tender will be accepted. In such situations, you owe one final letter to the candidate who has refused your offer. Your letter should be structured to keep the door open for future employment possibilities and also maintain positive public relations.

Model Letter 3-16

Dear _____:

I want to thank you for your interest in our sales position. I respect your decision to remain with your present organization and wish you success in pursuing your career goals.

As we discussed, I believe your experience and abilities would have suited you for a successful career with our growing sales organization.

If circumstances should change in the future, I would be interested in again discussing with you the employment opportunities in our company.

Sincerely,

4. WELCOMING THE NEW EMPLOYEE TO THE ORGANIZATION

When a candidate accepts your employment offer, it really is an occasion for celebration for both you and your new salesperson. For your part, you should feel certain that you have obtained the services of an individual who may become the top sales producer in your region or the entire company. Your new salesperson found a sales position he/she felt was perfect, an opportunity for work that would be both interesting and challenging, a chance to earn more than ever before. This salesperson set out to win that job and succeeded in getting it. That's cause for celebration. So celebrate — make the welcome aboard letter a sincere and happy communication.

Model Letter 3-17

Dear _____ :

Congratulations! It is a pleasure to welcome you.

I speak for our entire sales force in assuring you that **(a)** you have made a wise decision and joined the most progressive sales organization in the industry. I wish you success and happiness and a long career with _____ Corp.

I look forward to working with you. Be assured I will do everything in my power to help you realize your full potential and reach your most ambitious career goals. And we'll have fun doing it!

We're glad to have you with us. I look forward to getting started in a week.

Sincerely,

Alternate Wording:

(a) I know I speak for all of your new associates here when I wish you success, happiness, and a long, distinguished career with the most progressive sales organization in the industry.

4

MODEL LETTERS THAT WILL SELL YOUR SALESPEOPLE ON NEW POLICIES

4

MODEL LETTERS THAT WILL SELL YOUR SALESPEOPLE ON NEW POLICIES

"Employees resist change!" It's almost a management cliché. Perhaps a cliché but not a truth. Salespeople change the style of their clothes. They buy new cars, begin playing tennis instead of golf, change the style and length of their hair. Salespeople welcome change in their private lives and leisure activities. So why should they resist change at work? Maybe they don't resist change per se, but rather *resist being changed*.

You can't order change — you must sell it. If you expect your salespeople to make changes you request and to adapt new policies and procedures, you must convince them that it is to their advantage to change. That's not so bad when you stop to think about it. The sales manager's talent, his stock-in-trade, is persuasion. It's the same type of selling the manager enjoyed when back in the territory — and it can be as much fun.

1. ANNOUNCING A PRICE INCREASE AND SELLING THE BENEFITS

Oh yes. The same old product that was a bear to sell last year at X dollars is now going to sell for X dollars plus 5%. Remember the feeling when you were a sales rep? But the sky never fell, the customers never hung you from the highest light fixture as you were sure they would. As a matter of fact, at income tax time next year it usually turned out that the price increase had contributed to a pleasant increase in commissions earned. But somehow you forgot about that the next time a price increase was announced and the same doubts and fears recurred.

This is a tough one and worthy of an individual letter to the different types of salespeople on your staff. We'll look at a model letter aimed at the "comer" on your sales force, the person who started to blossom last year and should be gaining confidence daily. A different approach is needed for the hard-to-motivate, "average" producer on your sales staff (who lives conservatively and whose spouse works just to keep their income from falling below "X" dollars). The hard-nosed old pro who's going to retire in a few years (and she's been stashing it away for 20 years now) is a special case. This individual can make the difference in the national sales contest *when she wants to*. She can produce average sales working half days (and usually does). She turned down a promotion to sales management once because she "couldn't afford to take the cut." Many of her customers are better friends of hers than you are. Now how are you going to get her to sell this price increase?

One form letter to all sales reps announcing the increase just won't cut it. This deserves a special approach to each type.

Model Letter 4-1

Dear _____:

I do not claim that the new prices (price list attached) will make this year's selling easier than last year's. However, it is worth noting that if your unit sales this year are exactly the same as last year, you will earn approximately $1,600 more in commissions just as a result of the price increase.

We are both aware of some favorable factors which **(a)** will result in improved unit sales this year. Our 4% price increase gives us an even greater advantage over our major competition who just announced a 6% increase. Market conditions are improving almost daily in our industry, our customers are returning to their aggressive, expansion-minded ways after last year's uncertainty — they're in a buying mood again!

The most important factor, I believe, is additional **(b)** skill you gained and toughness you showed in last year's adverse selling conditions. The $1,600 additional commission is automatic, and I know you won't stop there with just equaling last year's unit sales.

Sincerely,

Alternate Wording:

(a) This isn't our first price increase nor will it be our last. Let's consider for a moment what we have going for us that will help us to sell more despite the increase. To begin with there's the new model that represents all plus business. And our new adjustment policy has already proven to be a business-maker. Finally, the new advertising program is bringing in new leads every day.

(b) Although price increases are unpleasant, I know from past experience you will make the most of the advantages you have at your disposal and will minimize the increase. That's the proper direction to take and the one that will insure that you will be enjoying at the very minimum that $1,600 increased commission at the end of the year.

Model Letter 4-2

Dear _____:

This should be the year for each of us to reach new sales heights!

Our customers are in a buying mood again now that **(a)** last year's uncertainty is behind them. Our major competitor has raised prices 6% across the board and I just got word that our new prices will be held to a 4%

increase (price list attached). This means two things to you — your price advantage over competition just became even bigger than last year and you just got an increase of $1,200 in commissions earned if your unit sales remain the same as last year. But with the improved business climate in our industry and the even more favorable price advantage over competition, you'll probably increase your unit sales by 10% this year. And that means another $1,620 in commissions.

So use the advantages we've got going for us this year and make that additional $2,800 in commissions. We both know you can do it.

Sincerely,

Alternate Wording:

(a) The industry has just announced a 6% increase in prices effective the first of the month. We are following suit and I have attached a new price list. That means you will enjoy an increase of $1,200 in commissions earned if your unit sales remain the same as last year.

But since prices are a valid comparison only against what competition is offering for the same product, you can see that we enjoy the same sales advantages as before the increase. So there is every reason to anticipate that you will enjoy the same sales increase you planned before the price increase — only now you will earn more while doing it.

The price increase combined with your planned increase in sales will result in $2,800 in increased commissions. Sound great? You betcha. And I know you can bring it off.

Model Letter 4-3

Dear _____:

You just got a raise, Ed. I've attached the new price list to this note. You'll notice that the increases have been held to 4%. That means your commissions earned for the coming year will increase by $1,400 on the same unit sales as last year.

Now I know you usually have figured out what the company is going to do before they give me the word. So you're probably as surprised as I am that the prices haven't been increased by 6%. Well, our increase is just part of the news, Ed. Our major competitor just increased their prices 6% across the board. So now you have an even wider price advantage. And I know while you were reading the past few lines you already thought of another two or three accounts you've been warming up for a long time who won't be able to say no to the even bigger price advantage you can now offer. That should bring your increased commissions up to $3,000 or more.

So go get them. Sell quality and service and then use the price advantage for the clincher — just like you always do. I only wish I could be there to see how you do it.

Sincerely,

2. ANNOUNCING IMPROVED PRICES OR TERMS AND SELLING THE BENEFITS

When we have good news for our sales force we may sometimes feel the advantages are so obvious they don't require emphasis or explanation. When we fall into that trap we risk losing some of the additional business we would get if we used all of the motivational power contained in the good news. A single explanation or announcement won't do when improved prices or terms are involved. Translate the improved prices or terms into potential sales increases. Use colorful cartoon letterheads where appropriate. Make it a celebration.

Model Letter 4-4

Dear _____:

Get your prospect list out before you read any more of this letter.

Got it out? Now go through your prospect list and see how many "hot ones" you could close if you could offer them these terms:

| | | Seasonal Savings |
Order Date	Shipment Date	Off List Price
11/15-12/08	12/31-02/28	5.5%
12/11-12/31	01/31-03/31	4.5%

Yes, we've finally got it! A cure for the "holiday **(a)**
put-off" and the December "see me after the first of
the year" blues!

We've got the closing tool we need to make December
a season to be jolly — and prosperous! Let's use this
sales tool to do just that. Let's not use it for an opener
and give away our advantage in the close. We know
that we have to sell the advantages of the big ticket
product like ours before the discount will sway the
buyer.

But what an effect these terms should have on a lot of
those buyers on your "hot list"!

We've got the extra edge we've been wanting. You
know how to use it — so let's get out and make this
holiday season a sales celebration!

Sincerely,

Alternate Wording:

(a) Yes, we've finally got it! The discount that will make us
completely competitive even with those few wholesalers that
have been underbidding us.

What a tremendous tool this will be. Use it where you know
price is a deciding factor. But don't give away profit (or
commissions) unnecessarily.

(a) Yes, we've finally got it! The closing tool that will make the
most procrastinating prospect want to move now. What
prospect can pass up the opportunity to make an extra 5.5%.
And since he has to buy now to get the discount, it makes a
perfect reason to act now.

3. ANNOUNCING A TERRITORY REALIGNMENT

"If I had that piece of Zone 4 that cuts into my territory, I'd outsell
John. That should be part of my territory. And that old section I've got
down by the expressway — why those old buildings are mostly vacant and

the few little mom-and-pop operations in there are losers. And the few office buildings left are full of answering services."

Sound familiar? The grass is always greener. Is there a way to convince all your salespeople that everybody wins and nobody loses as a result of the territory realignment? Individual phone conversations and face-to-face meetings may be called for to sell the benefits. However, written communication will be an absolute necessity to define the new boundaries, quotas, and advantages of the change to each salesperson.

Model Letter 4-5

Dear _____ :

You finally convinced me! You know that corner of territory 9 next to yours that you've mentioned to me several times? Well, it's now part of your territory. The northwest boundary of your territory is now the corner of Roosevelt Road (on the north) and Harlem Avenue (on the west) and the southwest boundary is the corner of Harlem Avenue (on the west) and 63rd Street (on the south).

I've attached a new territory map and you'll notice all of the industrial area you wanted around the airport is included. You'll also notice the old southern corner of your area has been made part of territory 8. I know you had two or three good prospects in that area and one or two good accounts. However, as you told me several times, a large portion of that corner consisted of parks, golf course, and the college.

I've attached a partial list of prospects and accounts in the new section of your territory. This list is based mainly on John's old call report cards and certainly isn't complete. Let's meet at the office next Monday at 8 a.m. and go over the territory map with a cross-reference directory and some of our prospecting tools and spend the rest of the day calling on several of the accounts and look the territory over.

The market index for that section is much higher than it was for the old section we transferred to territory 8. The quota is higher, of course, but you'll have no trouble exceeding it with the potential there.

After looking at the figures, I can see why you've been wanting this area.

See you Monday at 8:00 a.m.

Sincerely,

4. EXPLAINING WHY A SALES REP CANNOT HAVE A DESIRED TERRITORY REALIGNMENT

A territory realignment desired by the sales representative is not always possible or desirable. Refusing a territory realignment can become a sensitive issue when the salesperson takes the refusal to be a slap at his ability to handle the territory in question. Although the salesperson is refused, he should be encouraged to feel positive about his job, territory, and sales performance.

This is one of those situations in which it is frequently best to explain in person or by telephone that you are refusing the request. At the same time a letter follow-up is generally useful as a means to clarify the reasons for the refusal and to provide a record in the event conditions change.

The following letter provides a useful model for refusing realignment requests while retaining the sales rep's positive feelings about his territory.

Model Letter 4-6

Dear _____:

I'm sure you recognize that I would have made the territory change you requested if it were in your best interest and that of the company and the other sales rep. As we discussed by phone there are a number of considerations to your request.

1. The territory segment in question represents **(a)** a sizeable potential. Although that segment has not been developed to date, goals and plans have been established to do so. Bill is working hard to get things going there.

2. The market primarily represented in that segment is markedly different from that of your territory. That would require you to develop new marketing strategies. And al-

though I am sure you are up to that, I am not sure the extra effort is in the best interest of the company.

3. The segment in question would require an hour's driving time just to reach the area. That is time away from face-to-face selling and the productive use of your time.

Now let's focus on your own territory. I recognize you would like to have the increased territory to improve your own sales and income. That goal is commendable. Since we can't increase the geographical size of your territory, let's examine how you might be able to reach the same goal with your present territory. The territory segment in question has a sales potential of $120,000 per year. If you were able to get 25% of that potential the first year, you would be doing a good job. That would mean an additional $30,000 in sales. Here is my challenge. I believe you have the opportunity to increase sales by more than $30,000 in your present territory with the right plan and probably with less effort than it would take to cultivate the territory segment in question. Why don't you develop a plan of action for developing the wholesale segment of your present territory? That segment has a rich potential and has been relatively untouched in your area to date. According to our present figures that would have a greater potential and might readily provide the increase you seek.

I will await your plan of action. If you could have it ready by our next sales meeting the first of the month, I will take the time to review it with you so we might come to some mutual agreement as to how you might reach your goal.

In the meantime, Bill, thanks for your interest in the Northwest territory. Your desire for that segment shows you are thinking about growth and new horizons.

Sincerely,

Alternate Wording:

(a) Although the territory segment in question is closer geographically to yours, it represents a considerably different type of market.

(a) The overriding factor in this decision is that the sales rep calling on the accounts there has been in the territory for a number of years and is well-known and established in the area.

(a) The territory segment you request has only limited potential. The driving required to service the area will result in a high cost per dollar of business achieved.

5. REDUCING A SALES REPRESENTATIVE'S TERRITORY

"You break your neck to build up a territory, finally get everything rolling and making the good buck — and the so and so's cut your territory." Lines from "Death of a Salesman"? No. Lines from a sales rep's gripe session in the corner coffee shop, right? If you never said anything like that when you were a sales rep, you're the exception.

They have a point, don't they? That is how it looks sometimes from the sales rep's point of view. But the sales rep's territory isn't cut to limit her income. After all, the more she makes the more the company makes.

A sales manager may reduce the size of a sales rep's territory because he's spending too much effort on a marginal area in the territory and too little effort on the most promising part, thereby lowering his production and income. Or she may reduce the sales rep's territory because he's spending too much time driving and too little time face-to-face with prospects and customers — lowering production and income. The manager may take an area out of a sales rep's territory because the majority of the prospects and customers in that part are different than the bulk of customers and he has consistently been unable to adjust to the different sales approach needed to create customers in that area. So a territory reduction is for the sales rep's own good and he ought to welcome it rather than resist it.

"I'm reducing your territory but it will result in increased sales and earnings for you." Again, remember how you would have reacted to that when you were in a territory. A sales rep feels that his territory is his private property, his fiefdom. When you change the boundaries he will more likely react with emotion rather than reason, similar to the reaction you would have if the town you live in told you they were going to build an expressway through your backyard for your own good. When the change in territory boundaries means a net reduction in area, you can't expect the salesperson to be anything but disappointed, defensive and perhaps even hostile.

Your best persuasive powers are needed both face-to-face and in writing. The persuasion will be most effective if you have analyzed the territory with the sales rep and discussed with her possible ways of increasing sales in the territory including the possibility of relieving her of the responsibility for covering the marginal areas so she can concentrate on that with the greatest potential.

If the announcement of a cut in territory size comes to the sales rep in a letter with no prior discussion or consultation, there is a good chance she will take it as a personal insult and become a real management problem for you.

Model Letter 4-7

Dear _____:

I've given a lot of thought to the ideas we discussed last month. I agree with you that you've done a tremendous job in cracking the paper mills and related accounts in and around _____ city. I also believe you are right in anticipating even more new accounts and additional business from recent customers in that area. You definitely have found the key to that business.

I've also been going over your call reports for the last few months and some of my own notes to you regarding number of calls and accounts called upon. It appears I may have been getting in the way of your tapping the full sales potential of your territory. For instance, several times I asked why you hadn't called on _____ Company recently. A few weeks later I was questioning why the number of calls per day you were making had fallen off. After studying the map and remembering the roads in that part of the territory, it seems to me I've put you in an unreasonable predicament. I've been expecting you to service the few old accounts over in _____ and bring in new business over there.

But the real business is in _____ city and surrounding areas. So I'm removing _____ from your territory and therefore freeing you from the responsibility of servicing the old, unproductive accounts down there. If we left the territory the way it was, you would bring in additional business down there and increase the amount of your sales time there at the expense of bigger sales around _____ city.

You are now free to concentrate your sales efforts on the real "mother lode." I'm confident your sales and commissions will increase. Give it some thought and let's discuss your plans for really breaking it loose in the _____ city area when you phone in Monday morning.

Sincerely,

6. ANNOUNCING A NEW PRODUCT

"If you aren't sold on your product you can't sell it to anyone else," is a time-honored sales truism. When a new product is introduced, the sales manager's first job is to sell it to his salespeople. A description of the features of the new product or service won't sell the sales force. They'll get that from the brochures and sales aids provided. What will it do for their prospects and for them? The emphasis must be on the sales opportunity.

Model Letter 4-8

Dear _____:

This is our day!

With everything we've got going for us right now, **(a)** what one addition to our product line would you like to have to make this the perfect sales situation?

You told us. Back in November at the annual sales meeting, what did you ask for?

You've got it!

The _____ Super Shuttle Feeder opens sales opportunities with that large group of prospects who require a center loading feature.

This is the sales rep's dream — all the market conditions are right and the home office heard your request for the product you need to put it all together!

You've got it!

The time is right — the product is right — the *price* is right (see attached).

This is the situation you've dreamed about. A starter supply of brochures is attached. Order blanks are attached. Send them back filled in!

We know this new product is the key to record sales in a perfect market situation. You invented it — you've got it — enjoy it and sell!

Sincerely,

Alternate Wording:

(a) After nine months of research and field testing, here is a new product with proven customer need and appeal. In our initial field test, 84% of the customers surveyed reacted favorably to the benefits of our new Super Shuttle Feeder. Fifteen of them wanted to place orders immediately.

7. ANNOUNCING PRODUCT MODIFICATIONS

When you announce a change in the product line or modification of existing products, it will more likely be welcomed if communication like this precedes the change.

Model Letter 4-9

Dear _____:

The time is rapidly approaching to begin work on the 19__ model lineup. As you well know, _____ has long relied on dealers for ideas to help formulate our model line, and with economic conditions as they are today it is very important that we have a line that will be very saleable next year.

Since you and your salespeople are on the firing line 100% of the time, you are best equipped to provide us with information on what is needed right now to maximize sales. We will appreciate your help with answers to the following questions, plus adding any thoughts you have:

1. What new models are needed for 19___?
2. What equipment changes should be made on the 19___ models?
3. What color changes or additions should be made next year?
4. What models should be dropped?
5. What items of equipment make certain models more saleable than the competition's?

Please check with your salespeople to get their thoughts and please also pass along your own ideas on the 19___ models.

Thanks for your help.

Sincerely,

An announcement of product modification should stress the inherent market opportunities and refer to the part the sales force had in suggesting the change — if this is the case.

Model Letter 4-10

Dear _____:

In response to requests from many dealers, Silver Mist will be available on the following models effective immediately: Continental models 320, 322, and 326 and Sprint models 422 and 424. Sky Blue will be added to model J38-9 and J38-6 Sting Rays.

These additional colors on Continentals, Sprints, and   **(a)**
Sting Rays should enhance sales considerably, and in many cases lead to plus business.

Sincerely,

Alternate Wording:

(a) Our market research work has confirmed your feelings that the customer wants a greater color selection in our product line. So here it is. Use it to get that sale that is sitting on the fence.

8. ANNOUNCING A NEW SALES AID AND SELLING THE BENEFITS

If the sales rep doesn't believe the new sales aid will help make the sale, you can bet it won't — because the prospect will never see it.

An efficient and worthwhile sales tool won't necessarily sell itself. Be sure your introduction tells how to use the sales aid most effectively and points out types of sales situations where the sales tool applies.

Model Letter 4-11

Dear _____:

A powerful new sales aid is now available. It is an owner testimonial record bound in a jacket and printed with hard-hitting sales messages. To produce the record, on-farm interviews were made with enthusiastic owners in ten different states — Pennsylvania, New York, Michigan, Indiana, Illinois, Wisconsin, Minnesota, Iowa, Kansas, and Oklahoma. Each 8-inch record is recorded on both sides with ten minutes of dairy testimonials on the front and ten minutes of beef information on the "flip side." The record is narrated by _____, well-known farm broadcaster. On both the dairy and beef sides, a number of points are made in the actual words of owners. Less labor, lower field losses, better livestock production . . . all these points are made again and again backed up with actual owner experience. The record is bound in an attractive folder which contains additional information about _____, including tax advantages and reasons to "buy now." It comes in an envelope suitable for mailing.

Here is what we recommend you do:

1. Become familiar with the contents of the record and jacket.

2. Mail a record to your best prospects. Then schedule a follow-up call with each prospect to discuss how the prospect can enjoy the benefits of _____ farming referred to on the record jacket and by _____ owners on the record.

3. When a first call reveals a qualified prospect, leave a copy of the record for the prospect to play prior to the next scheduled contact.

4. Use the record at fairs to get new prospects. Play the testimonials over a public address system at your display. Announce that the record is available to those who request it. Record request cards can be distributed for follow-up.

You will want to start using this new sales aid right away. The record is available for immediate shipment in lots of 100 at $3.50 each. Tapes are available for use at fairs in cassette form or reel-to-reel at $7.50 each.

Sincerely,

Here's an additional letter which introduces a sales aid through the dealer organization. Notice how it uses the dealer as a valuable link in the communication chain.

Model Letter 4-12

Dear _____:

Hogs are beautiful — about $20 more beautiful than they have been in the past.

Attached is a copy of the new _____ Swine Feeding Handbook. The new feeding handbook will be mailed to your salespeople August 6.

You may wish to discuss the new feeding handbook with your sales reps in a dealership sales meeting soon after that date. We have attached five feeding problems and the solutions if you wish to include a practice session in using the tables in the handbook to fill animal nutritional requirements in your sales meeting.

Notice, too, that tables 3 and 4 provide examples of typical diets. We believe this handbook contains all of the information your salespeople need not only in conventional sales situations but also anything they might need when it gets tough and complex.

Your sales force can provide a valuable service to their customers and increase sales by using this sales tool.

Sincerely,

5

LETTERS TO EXTEND THE EFFECTIVENESS OF YOUR SALES CONTESTS

5

LETTERS TO EXTEND THE EFFECTIVENESS OF YOUR SALES CONTESTS

When you put together a sales contest, you create a fantasy world, a Disney World. In the imaginative world of your contest, sales people will make calls from 7:00 a.m. to 9:00 p.m. to win a necktie or scarf with the company logo — because that identifies them to the rest of the sales force as the elite top 10% of the sales force. Of course, a trip to Hawaii should accompany that symbol. The artificial world of a sales contest is fragile. Just as an unobtrusive army of behind-the-scenes workers keep Disney World "real" by keeping everything functioning perfectly, the sales manager must provide continuity and constant communication of standings so that the sales force knows the situation in their contest world at every moment and each one cares what there position is in relation to the other contestants.

The success of a sales contest is largely due to the amount of excitement and enthusiasm generated. The awards for winning contribute to that excitement. But a constant stream of communication to inform, motivate and reward all participants is what makes performance matter to the salespeople. A proven way to get the job done is with well-written and imaginative letters. The sales contest consists of three phases: the launching in which rules and awards are announced, the work phase, and finally the payoff. Each phase makes its own demands on the sales manager to motivate and guide the sales force. The model letters that follow are organized in these three categories for your convenient use.

Many sales managers like to use prepared letterheads for their contest letters. These may be prepared specifically for the contest with contest name and slogan and perhaps colorful cartoons or illustrations. Envelopes can also be printed with matching identification. The reason for identification on the envelope and letterhead is to command the salesperson's attention from the second they spot the envelope in their mailbox — something special, news from the "real" world, the sales contest world. If budget won't allow investment in custom-designed, four-color letterheads for the contest, take a look at the wide selection of themes and illustrations offered by several companies.

Make it a policy during a contest to use some type of illustrative material on every communication you send out. Salespeople are action people. Put extra action in your contest communication to command attention. We have omitted the illustrations in the model letters because they must be carefully tailored to your situation and color is important and not practical here. But we have suggested where appropriate types of illustrative material would be useful.

1. ANNOUNCING THE SALES CONTEST

Whenever possible use a special meeting to kick off a sales contest. Such special attention provides the contest with the sense of importance and excitement required to generate enthusiasm in the sales force and focus their attention on the goals of the contest. But that is not always possible, is it? Your sales organization may be so widely scattered that bringing them together to announce a contest would use up a big piece of the contest budget. Or perhaps, as many sales managers do, you run contests on a rather continual basis, making a kickoff meeting for every contest impractical. Then letters are an excellent way to launch a contest. Each of the following letters was used for that purpose. Although the incentives and rules of the contest may vary from what you have planned, you will find considerable value in the various letters to build interest and add impact to your own announcements.

Model Letter 5-1

Dear _____:

ANNOUNCING THE ULTIMATE
FIRST-QUARTER SALES CONTEST.

You're gonna love this sales contest! It's got everything — the product, the price, the awards — everything you could want.

PRODUCT

Five products will count in the first quarter contest — the hot new Enterprise Line introduced last September. Your prospects and customers have already voted "yes" on this line with most encouraging volume for a brand new product. You know we've found an unfilled niche in the market with this line. We want to establish a broad customer base with strong first quarter sales and preclude the entry of "me too" product introductions from competition.

PRICE

We are temporarily providing you selective price **(a)** reductions from 2% to 9% across the model line for the first quarter only. This is to give your customers an even greater incentive to try this great new line. But please sell the benefits of the new line and save the discount for a closer.

AWARDS

Here is the payoff schedule for extra effort and results in the first quarter:

10% above quota in the *month*	—your choice of any item in section 1 of the enclosed prize book.
20% above quota in the *month*	—your choice of any item in section 2 of the enclosed prize book.

30% above quota in the *month*   —your choice of any item
in section 3 of the
enclosed prize book.

That's right — prize eligibility starts over the first
day of each month of the contest. You're never out of
contention. And what are the awards for outstanding
sales volume throughout the entire quarter?

10% over quota for first quarter — three days at   **(b)**
Caesar's Palace, Las Vegas with extra night club
show and tour packages, the ultimate no-sleep Las
Vegas grand tour.

20% over quota for first quarter — four days at the
Acapulco resort of Los Brisas — each suite has its
own swimming pool outside its own private patio at
this famous Mexican resort. And you also have your
own pink "Jeep" waiting at your door for sightseeing
or a side trip to the famous artist's village of Taxco or
a ride over to watch the cliff divers.

30% over quota for first quarter — a *one week*
Caribbean cruise on the luxurious Norwegian Cruise
Lines ship *Sunward II* with ports of call Nassau, Puerto
Rico, and St. Thomas, Virgin Islands.

The special discount price list for the first quarter is
attached and so are the prize catalogue and trip
brochures.

We'll discuss this further and I'll answer any questions during our regular Monday morning phone
call. I know you are as excited as I am about this great
first quarter contest.

Sincerely,

Alternate Wording:

(a) Customers have already shown that they recognize the value
of the new line by ordering it at an unusually rapid rate for a
new line. We want to provide you every advantage to keep
sales building. Therefore we are providing a temporary 5%
discount. Please don't use the discount as an opener to get
interest. Our experience has shown the discount will be most

helpful to you when held in reserve as an additional closing inducement after the prospect is basically sold on the product.

(b) You will win an exciting getaway vacation for yourself and a companion for superior volume for the entire first quarter. 10% over quota wins you a long weekend in Las Vegas, 20% over quota wins four days in Acapulco, and a 30% increase over the first quarter of last year gets you the vacation of a lifetime — a week-long Caribbean cruise to Nassau, Puerto Rico, and St. Thomas in the Virgin Islands on the NCL ship *Sunward II*. The brochures are enclosed.

Model Letter 5-2

Dear _____:

In 90 days you will have won the First Annual Northern Region Spring Sales Contest! How do I know you'll win? Because in this contest you can't lose.

In this contest you're playing your territory. And I know you are on top of your territory.

Here's how it works:

Territory II

April	Last year	8 units	This year's quota	10
May	Last year	10 units	This year's quota	12
June	Last year	6 units	This year's quota	8

You already knew that, right? So what's the contest? The contest is between you and your territory. Go over quota by just a unit each month and you're a winner!

What if you get off to a slow start and go under quota the first month but finish strong and end up three units over quota for the quarter? You win! Just finish out the quarter three units over quota to win.

What do you win?

Three units over quota wins three days, two nights in Las Vegas! The entire package includes round trip, all meals, accommodations and a night club tour. The enclosed brochure describes the trip in detail.

I'll phone on Monday to discuss any questions you may have and to double-check your prospect list. I want to be sure you're building a "hot list" that will make Las Vegas a sure thing.

Sincerely,

The writer illustrated this letter with a proliferation of money and checks around the border.

The following model letter introduces an incentive program that caters to the need for ego satisfaction by using the ever popular trophy.

Model Letter 5-3

Dear _____ :

The enclosed photograph was taken last year as our salesman of the year (name) received the traveling trophy from our company president (name) at our annual awards banquet. This same picture, you will recall, ran in the newspaper and in the company magazine with an accompanying article.

Who's going to be the winner this year? Will it be _____ again or will you pull out to win it? Perhaps one of the previous year's winners will come back as a two-time winner. At this point, every one of you is a likely candidate.

You will be pleased to know that the award will be made in Honolulu this year. That's right, you and a companion, if you are the winner, will be flown at company expense to receive your award under the swaying palms. The attached sheet provides the details.

OK, all you beach bums. Let's get with it. One of you is going to be a winner.

Sincerely,

Model Letter 5-4

Dear _____ :

HERE IS YOUR THREE-MONTH   (a)
SPECIAL ACHIEVEMENT BONUS PROGRAM.

This is the contest that can substantially increase your earnings. You can win prizes worth over $2,000, plus the extra commissions you'll earn. You'll have your choice of travel, merchandise, or cash.

During this contest last year Bill Holland won a trip for two to Rio de Janeiro. Andrea Spencer won a set of Wilson Staff golf clubs and bag, Dave Brown walked off with $850 cash.

This year the awards are bigger. The chances of big winnings are even greater. And with all we've got going for us this year, everyone can be a big winner. Details of the contest are attached. Take special note:

- Awards are larger than last year.
- Goals are based on the same percent increase as last year.
- There is a special extra bonus for the top sales producer in each product line.

I'll mail progress reports every week. Get off to a fast start; don't wait until the last minute to qualify for this great money-making opportunity.

STARTING DATE: Noon, Friday May 30

ENDING DATE: 9:30 a.m., Friday August 29

Sincerely,

Alternate Wording:

(a) TRY YOUR HAND AT SWEEPSTAKES POKER.

For one month only (June), we'll be playing poker. Every Model 630 sale entitles you to play one poker hand. Every Model 830 sale entitles you to play two hands of poker and a 960 sale keeps you in for three hands. Poker hands will be played each Friday based on that week's sales. The pot will be 1% of sales made divided evenly among hands played. (Letterhead used for this letter featured playing cards and cartoon card-playing scene.)

If you have other sales managers working for you, consider including them in the contest. They can make a big difference to the success of the contest and too often they are neglected. This letter was written for that purpose.

Model Letter 5-5

Dear _____:

Here's something on the side especially for you! We realize how important, you the sales manager, are to the success of any incentive program. So when your sales team reaches goal, you will receive a .5% bonus on all sales. When you reach 110% of goal you will receive .75% bonus on all sales. And should you be successful in reaching 120% of goal you will receive a full 1% bonus on all sales.

Are the opportunities for big money available to you? What do you think?

% of Quota	Here's What You Will Earn
100%	_____
110%	_____
120%	_____

The rules are simple. Just meet or break quota. The contest ends midnight, July 31.

Sincerely,

2. THE WORK PHASE

The worst thing that can happen to a sales contest is for the sales force to lose interest. That happens when we don't keep our salespeople constantly informed or when the spread in the standings becomes hopelessly wide — the contest is dominated by one or two individuals.

The second cause is often a reflection of poorly structured territories or account responsibilities and can be cured by restructuring territories to distribute prospects more evenly. *Or, if uneven territories are necessary to serve sophisticated large accounts with the most experienced salespeople, for instance, "handicap" rules in the contest can even out competition. For instance, class I territory $1 sales volume is equal to $1.50 sales volume in class II territory. Of course, the most effective contest design is generally thought to be each salesperson

---

* For specific methods of territory design, see the book *Successful Sales Management* by Hal Fahner; Prentice-Hall, Inc., 1983.

competing with his or her own previous percent of sales. So, sales management remedies are available to cure competitive imbalances.

We must keep our salespeople constantly informed of contest standings and anything that is happening which may affect them. Weekly reports of standings are a must. Tips on the hottest industries or types of prospects, "war stories" about the methods used by the front-runners, reminders to use certain sales aids or methods are all appropriate elements in our communication with the sales force during the contest. Many sales managers employ a weekly newsletter format to keep current standings in front of the sales force at all times and deliver sales tips to everyone. Letters to individual salespeople can help fine-tune the attitudes and sales approach of each member of your sales force.

Model Letter 5-6

Dear _____:

We are almost halfway through PLUS TWENTY. I like your chances for finishing in the money for the entire contest. And there is no reason you can't pick up an extra $400 next month by selling just two more units than you did last year. I know you agree that next month's bonus is well within your reach, so let's concentrate on your position in the overall quarter-long contest. Can you make the quarter? Consider this:

- You're already halfway there. With half the contest period remaining, you need approximately 12 average sales. You've had streaks of two to three sales per week for a couple of months without a dry week many times.

- Other salespeople have already qualified. This includes a couple of people you've been out-selling regularly all year. If they can do it, you can do it!

- You made it last year. You are a better salesperson now than you were last year.

Some of the highest producers across the country in   **(a)**
this contest have been using that new proposal format the sales support department introduced last month. I'd like to come out and go over it with you

and see if it would help with any of your current prospects. Set up some appointments where it might apply for next Tuesday and Wednesday and I'll plan on making calls with you those days. Phone me Friday and we'll work out the details.

Sincerely,

Alternate Wording:

(a) I'm sure you can make it. I'm so sure that I made a side bet with the V.P. of Marketing this morning. He noticed you weren't on target this year and he knows you always place high in contests. So I bet him $50 that you would finish in the money. That's how sure I am. How about it? Can you prove me right?

The following letter is suitable for the lower third in the standings early in the contest.

Model Letter 5-7

Dear _____:

Here is the latest in contests — The Great Turtle   **(a)**
Getaway. No, it didn't start out with that name, but a few of you slow starters are making that a proper label.

You have yet to get on the board, Linda. And I know you aren't satisfied with that. Big bonus bucks are at stake, not to mention your standing in the sales force.

Plenty of time remains. You can still make it to the front of the pack. Remember the tortoise and the hare?

Sell your shell off!

Sincerely,

Alternate Wording:

(a) Turtles seldom win anything. It took a fairy tale for one to win a race against a rabbit. It's time for the turtles to get out of the starting gate. There are big winnings at stake and I know you better than to believe you are satisfied with your present place in the standings.

The sales manager who wrote the above letter sent out a toy turtle with it and got the attention of the slow starters. It undoubtedly served as a constant reminder to the slow-start salespeople.

At the other end of the spectrum, salespeople who start out a contest with a hot streak can become complacent. This letter was intended to spur a contest leader to even greater accomplishment.

Model Letter 5-8

Dear _____:

Just great! Congratulations on the fastest start I've ever seen in the annual sales contest. It must feel great!

I don't want you looking over your shoulder to see if anyone's gaining on you. I'll do that, you just keep making the calls and the profit proposals. But, by the way, it's Sharon Weber in Hicksville, N.Y. who is off to the second fastest start I've ever seen. She's supposed to be a real comer. The N.Y.C. District Manager claims she's the smoothest closer he's had working for him in 20 years. Claims when she gets to the presentation stage with a prospect, it's all over, a sure sale. And the Long Island market has been the healthiest in the country all year.

But you are in a position to pull away from the field,   **(a)**
leave Weber and the rest wondering what happened. Don't slow down now. Your performance this quarter will become a company legend if you continue the pace you've set. Everyone in the office is excited. We're all behind you and want to see you leave New York in your dust. Any help we can provide is yours for the asking.

Sincerely,

Alternate Wording:

(a) Most races are won or lost in the stretch. Now's the time to give that procrastinating customer one more try. Now's the time to pull out a fresh approach to get an order from that tough prospect. The next month is crucial and you have the support of everyone in the district. We all want to beat New

York. Give me a call if you have anything hanging I might help with or sales support might help speed along.

If you market through dealers, this letter will be useful. It is actually a pair of letters — the first designed to motivate the dealer, the other the dealer's salespeople.

Model Letter 5-9

Dear _____ :

Dave and I just want to take a moment to thank you for your efforts in getting the "Getting Your Share" program off to an excellent start. With your leadership we know (*name of dealership*) will be getting its share plus. We have enclosed a letter from us to your employees expressing our thanks for superior performance. I hope you will send it on to them for us.

Thanks again for your outstanding management and leadership.

Sincerely,

Model Letter 5-10

To all employees (*name of dealership*):

We want to thank all of you for the outstanding results you produced in the first three weeks of the "Getting Your Share" sales contest. You are among the leaders for the entire country, where you belong. The idea of "Getting Your Share" is that if you give a little you will get a little more and that's a fact. "Getting Your Share" is for all of you. We know that all of you will get your share as you all continue the teamwork and cooperation you have demonstrated to this point in thc contest.

Sincerely,

Sales managers agree that a sales contest is more than a carrot and stick proposition today. A successful sales contest:

- Teaches better selling methods and rewards those who gain skill in using the new methods.

- Provides for sales training rather than depending upon extra selling time and effort only.

Salespeople will generally be more receptive to new ideas and methods during a contest, especially if a bonus or glory is in sight. This letter takes advantage of the receptivity of this special period.

Model Letter 5-11

Dear _____:

We're now one-third of the way through the annual sales contest. We are hanging onto *First Place* by our fingernails. Although we are now ahead of Los Angeles by $450,000, they've been within $20,000 of us twice in the first month of the contest. Sue Dunston is tied with a salesperson from Cleveland and another from L.A. for seventh in the U.S. and Charley Stern is in sixteenth place in his first year with the company. All of you are well ahead of last year in volume and individual contest standings. I want the office to win it all this year and each of you to finish high in individual standings.

We need an extra advantage to make a real breakthrough in the next month. We've got two new sales tools to help us set a new record in February:

1. We've got a mailing out to 400 purchasing agents at the top companies in the three industries you've identified as our best market right now.

2. Sales support has developed a simplified proposal form using many of the suggestions we gave them last spring.

We'll have a sales meeting *all day* next Monday to give you your prospect list from the mailing (average 40 prospects each) and show you how to follow up on all of them. We'll also learn how to utilize the new proposal form. We are being used as the test group on this sales tool, since so many of the ideas for simplifying it came from us. I "volunteered" us to sales support since I think we've all agreed the streamlined proposal will be easier to use and more   **(a)** meaningful to prospects. We're the only office to use this form at this time.

We're in first place, we've got a fresh batch of key prospects, and we've got a new profit proposal to use in closing sales! See you Monday — you'll leave here Monday afternoon with everything you need to set a record in February.

Sincerely,

Alternate Wording:

(a) Sales Support offered us the chance to be the "guinea pig" last spring when we gave them more suggestions and help than any other office. I didn't expect it to come back to help us in the middle of the annual contest, but I didn't think you'd mind this extra advantage.

The last days of a sales contest call for a little extra sales management effort. Many sales managers send a letter a day, sort of a play-by-play, the last two or three weeks. Some managers use telegrams and mailgrams the last week or two for an extra feeling of urgency and importance.

Model Letter 5-12

TELEGRAM

ONLY 10 DAYS LEFT IN "FLYING DOWN TO RIO." ALL STANDINGS CLOSE. AS LITTLE AS $5,000 MORE SALES WILL SEND MANY OF YOU TO BRAZIL. MAKE AN EXTRA CALL A DAY FOR NEXT TWO WEEKS — THEN HEAD FOR BERLITZ LANGUAGE LESSON AND THE TRIP OF YOUR LIFE!

Model Letter 5-13

TELEGRAM

LAST WEEK OF NATIONAL SALES CONTEST AND YOU ARE #1 — BUT WE DIDN'T HEAR MUCH FROM YOU LAST WEEK — ONLY 12 ORDERS — SAN FRANCISCO GAINING ON YOU

AFTER SENDING IN 26 — REPEAT — 26 ORDERS
LAST WEEK. YOU NEED A BIG WEEK TO HOLD
OFF THE CHALLENGE FROM THE WEST.

Individual competition can be a powerful motivator, whether between salespeople in the same office or across the country. You can encourage healthy competition with communication during a contest.

Model Letter 5-14

Dear _____:

You've heard that #2 tries harder? I'm afraid that may have happened last week. Thank you for the two orders. I appreciated the volume as this office overtakes Dallas to become #1 in the country.

But all of your fellow sales professionals in the Minneapolis office are pulling for you to win the national sales contest, an honor never before won by a representative from this office. Terry Boyce in Omaha brought in three orders last week closing the gap to only four orders between you in 1st and her in 2nd.

We all know you can do it! One more week, one more hot streak, and you'll have the honor of #1 in the sales force, and you will have given the Minneapolis office a new professional pride and spirit. You can do it!

Sincerely,

3. THE PAYOFF

At the completion of the contest, congratulations are in order. Congratulations are in order as far down the line as possible. The first year salesperson in a territory which had been "run down" by its last occupant may rightfully feel as much achievement in placing twentieth as the veteran in the same territory for several years feels in placing third.

Model Letter 5-15

Dear _____:

Congratulations! You are a winner in the "Extra Effort" sales contest. The results for each salesperson and prizes won is provided on the enclosed sheet.

Extra Effort has been a tremendous success. Sales during the contest increased by 37%, making this one of the best sales periods ever. This success was the result of the superb "Extra Effort" you gave to bring in those extra $_____ in sales. We couldn't have done it without you.

Thanks!

Sincerely,

Model Letter 5-16

Dear _____:

Congratulations on winning ninth place in the 19__ National Sales Contest. The 15 new contracts which you signed were an important contribution to the winning Detroit sales team.

I can only remember two other people finishing in the Top Ten in North America in their first year with the company, and they are now vice presidents. I look forward to following your career with us. I know you will set many other records.

Congratulations again on your outstanding accomplishment.

Sincerely,

6

LETTERS THAT MOLD YOUR SALES TEAM TOGETHER DURING TOUGH TIMES

6

LETTERS THAT MOLD YOUR SALES TEAM TOGETHER DURING TOUGH TIMES

Every sales manager would like to feel his sales force is a team working toward a common cause. Each member of the team is concerned for the welfare of the other. Management helps sales representatives. Sales reps are the right arm of management. When such a team exists the result will be a sales force that works harder to achieve common goals and is willing to sacrifice for the common good.

But what happens when the going gets tough? What happens when deliveries are slow, when service problems develop, or customary services must be reduced? At such times it becomes too easy for sales reps to blame "those people back at the home office." Managers are tempted to deny a problem even exists, at least with their sales force. The result is disaster. Now we are reduced to fault-finding and stonewalling — a miniature Watergate with similar effect.

We live in a new age. People feel they can think for themselves if they are given necessary information. When the home office responds with a "Problem? What Problem?" attitude, salespeople are likely to feel that management doesn't understand their problems or doesn't care. Or worse yet, they feel that management is too ignorant to cope with the situation.

Sales managers today recognize the futility of pretending all's right with the world when the company is facing a delivery crisis or other temporary but serious setback. These managers realize that their salespeople are among the first to become aware of such problems. They also recognize that their sales reps are capable of dealing with such problems if they are adequately informed.

Salespeople generally are not asking the company to solve all problems within 24 hours. Rather, they want to know what the situation is, what general approach management expects them to follow during the crisis, what specific methods they are expected to use, and what end results they are expected to achieve if these things differ from previously agreed upon plans. Sales reps, by the very nature of their daily activity, are more familiar than anyone in the company with the effect the company problem is having on the customer. Sales management should therefore invite the sales rep's participation in continuing efforts to improve the situation. Immediately useable, pragmatic solutions might result.

Telephone communications are vital to the line manager during such problem times. But written communication provides extra impact to remind both sales force and management of the goals and procedures agreed upon.

These are difficult letters to write. A negative, defeatist tone in the correspondence is deadly and can be counted on to produce a "morale problem" in the sales force. But an unrealistic "there's no problem" tone can have an equally devastating effect. The model letters that have been included in this section provide a positive approach to the problem while:

1. Recognizing the situation or defining the problem.
2. Explaining the general approach the company expects of the sales force during this period.
3. Making specific assignments to the sales reps.
4. Inviting sales rep participation in continuing efforts to improve the situation.

This section is organized according to the types of home office problems you are likely to encounter. Each section provides not only a letter from the sales manager to his salespeople, but an additional letter from the general sales manager to his line managers. As you will note the problems and communication approach is different for each.

1. EXPLAINING DELIVERY DELAYS AND EMPHASIZING POSITIVE SALES APPROACH

Making the sale is tough enough under ordinary circumstances. But when a sales rep has done all the hard work of making the sale and late delivery forces the rep to "mend his fences" once or even twice, morale is bound to be affected. If sales management knows delivery delays may continue for a period of time, communication with the sales force is necessary.

Model Letter 6-1
(From the chief sales officer to line sales managers)

Dear _____:

As you know, delivery delays have recently become a factor in our selling. The production people are working to correct this situation.

Their efforts will undoubtedly produce improved delivery in the near future. However, I believe it is realistic to take probable delivery delays into consideration in our marketing plans for the next six months.

From a marketing standpoint I am determined that we achieve three main objectives in the next six months: **(a)**

1. Maintain our largest and most profitable customers. We are establishing an allocation and priority system (details sent under separate cover) to insure that competitors do not gain an advantage with our established accounts.

2. Continue to gain new key accounts. The priority system will provide for orders from new key accounts.

3. Gain orders for future delivery and accustom our customers to this kind of planned and

organized purchasing. Customers' incentives (discounts) are provided in our allocation and priority system to encourage this planned approach to purchasing which will benefit both our customers and us.

Take the following steps with your sales force within the next two weeks:

a. Explain the delivery situation is temporary and will begin to improve shortly, but the problem will not be completely resolved for approximately six months. Do not be apologetic and do not place blame on "those production people." This situation is partly due to successful selling by your sales force and a high quality product.

Success, growth, and expansion often bring problems such as delivery delays. There is no need to fix blame, but there is a need to convince your salespeople that this is a "good problem" which need only be a minor irritation as they continue to increase their sales and their incomes.

b. Explain our three main marketing objectives — maintain volume of major accounts, gain new accounts, sign solid orders for future delivery rather than immediate delivery.

c. Reach agreement on specific goals with each of your sales reps in each of these areas. Use an incentive contest among your salespeople based on meeting and exceeding these goals or any other device you wish.

d. Invite suggestions from your salespeople which will help accomplish our three main marketing objectives for the next six months.

I expect a report from you within two weeks outlining your specific goals for your sales office in each of the three main marketing objective areas.

I realize emphasis on large, profitable accounts will be necessary to reach our goals and we may miss some business from smaller marginal accounts during this crucial period. But we can continue our sales growth during the next six months and be in an even stronger position in each sales territory when delivery capability returns to normal six months from now.

I know your salespeople will view this period as a time of sales opportunity if we clearly present the job to be done.

Sincerely,

Alternate Wording:

(a) Your sales organization must provide the greatest care to communicate with your customers during this period. Customers will accept delivery delays only when they are forewarned to expect them and know when to expect their end. This means your salespeople have a special job during the next six months to keep our customers fully informed of the progress of our delivery situation and to inform them of what they can do to minimize the impact of such delays.

The sales manager is now prepared to communicate the problem and company solution to his sales force. Certain definite action and results are needed from the sales reps. Informing them is not enough. They must be convinced that the action they are instructed to take is in their own best interest and will result in maximum sales and income for them under present circumstances. Face-to-face meetings with the sales reps individually or in groups will be necessary. Two-way communication, discussion of the situation, the activities they are to perform, the results they must produce — is a necessity. Just informing the sales reps risks silent disagreement and resistance from them. A cynical, defeatist attitude in the sales force will be disastrous. This letter was used to prepare them for the face-to-face meeting.

Model Letter 6-2
(From the line sales manager to his sales force)

Dear _____:

As you know, delivery delays have recently become a factor in our selling. The production people are working to correct this situation and their efforts will undoubtedly produce improved delivery in the near future. This situation is due in large measure to your effective selling and our high quality product. It is a "good problem" that often accompanies growth, expansion, and success.

The Vice President of Marketing has set four major   **(a)**
objectives for the next six months — maintain our largest and most profitable customers, continue to gain new key accounts, gain orders for future delivery, and accustom our customers to this kind of planning and organized purchasing.

To help us reach these objectives an allocation and priority system for orders will be instituted immediately. A customer incentive or discount program is also being introduced immediately to enable us to sign orders for future delivery. In other words, we are being given the sales tools we need to maintain our fast pace.

We will have a meeting at the office next Monday morning to discuss these new sales tools and plan for their effective use.

Please prepare for our meeting by reviewing your present customers and prospects. Be prepared to list your key accounts and key prospects. Also think about how you can use the customer incentive program to sign orders for future delivery and which accounts will be most receptive to this program.

Sincerely,

Alternate Wording:

(a) During the next six months we must maintain our largest and most profitable customers, continue to gain new key accounts, gain orders for future delivery, and accustom our customers to this kind of planning and organized purchasing.

Model Letter 6-3
(From the chief sales offices to line sales managers)

Dear _____:

As you know, orders for our recently introduced sprayer model #___ have been coming in at a rate even higher than we anticipated. Our customers are recognizing and clamoring for the built-in advantages that our three-way mixing ratio sprayer provides.

Demand has been so great we are having difficulty filling all orders. One part, supplied by a vendor, is in short supply and we do not presently have an alternate source. I anticipate the shortage situation will continue for at least 90 days.

I am pleased with the reception this product has **(a)** received in the market and concerned at the possibility of losing sales due to short supply. However, I'm not sure that we must lose sales. Several other products in our line will perform a similar function to the model #____, although I recognize that they do not include some of the features of this model.

I suggest you emphasize to your sales force the need to determine from the buyer exactly what application is required and then ask themselves what alternative products in our line will do that job. I must concede that in some situations only our model #____ would satisfy the customer. In those situations the sales representative must convince the customer that the model #____ is worth waiting for and make the sale on a back-order basis.

I believe your salespeople will get the job done. In the meantime, our production people are doing everything they can to catch up with the demand.

Sincerely,

Alternate Wording:

(a) We have initiated an emergency order system to take effect immediately. It works like this. We are holding back a small stock of sprayers to supply dealers who are completely out of stock or are in immediate danger of running out. In those situations we will draw from our emergency stock as long as it lasts.

Five units is the maximum order we can honor for delivery from emergency stock. I'm sure you realize that this system won't work if it is abused. It is designed for the true emergency condition. If your salespeople order out of the emergency stock for regular stock replenishment, the supply will soon be depleted.

To secure stock from the emergency supply, your sales representatives should mark their orders "Emergency Stock."

Model Letter 6-4
(From the line sales manager to his sales force)

Dear _____:

I remember thinking one day after a sales call on a particularly hard-nosed prospect, "I wish the day would come when sales were so good that he couldn't buy my product no matter how badly he wanted it."

Well, that day seems to be here with the new model #____ and it isn't fun like I expected it to be. I know you feel the same way.

The recently introduced sprayer model #____ has been selling as well across the country as it has here. A vendor-supplied part is in short supply and a back-order situation has developed. I've been assured that the factory people are doing everything they can to catch up with demand, but for the present we are in a back-order situation.

However, our sales don't have to suffer. There are at least two things we can do. We have a unique, high quality product superior to anything competition can offer with this new model. We should be able to convince the buyer that it is worth waiting for rather than buying from competition. Also we can work harder to determine from the buyer exactly what application is required and then ask ourselves what other products in our line will do the job. I suspect in many cases we will find that we can satisfy the customer's requirements with one of our products. You know, our sales of several other models have fallen off since the model #____ was introduced.

Let's get together Monday and discuss it. You've got

(a)

some ideas on keeping sales as high as they've been, I know.

Sincerely,

Alternate Wording:

(a) We can maintain our high level of sales by convincing the buyer that our product is worth waiting for. We can also do a better job of determining exactly what function the product will perform and then ask ourselves what other products in our line will do that job.

2. EXPLAINING SERVICE PROBLEMS AND EMPHASIZING POSITIVE SALES APPROACH

One of the items that most companies are selling along with their product is their service on that product. When service breaks down the quality of the package of values that the sales rep is selling is diminished. Complaints multiply. The sales representative's job becomes infinitely more difficult. Your sales force can handle the problem of poor service if they know the problem is temporary, that steps are being taken to correct the problem and when it is likely to be corrected. The following letters tell the sales force what action the company is going to take and what action is expected of the sales representative.

Model Letter 6-5
(From the chief sales officer to line sales managers)

Dear _____ :

You and your salespeople are right. Our service capability has fallen behind the sales force. Customer complaints are evidence that immediate action must be taken to bring customer service up to an acceptable level.

The Service Department Manager has promised to hire additional service reps and buy additional modern equipment for faster and better quality work on each service call. Also, he is beginning a training program on servicing the newest products for all service personnel. Please communicate these improvements to your salespeople.

We are setting up a "hotline" system to minimize customer problems during the period it will take to get service back to the high level we all expect. The purpose of the "hotline" system is to prevent any customer from having his production shut down because he can't get service from us. The details of the plan are attached. Note that we have divided service calls into four categories. Those situations which could give us a "black eye" in the market if mishandled receive top priority. Explain this system to your sales reps and be sure they know how to use it with their customers. If the sales reps "cheat" and attempt to get top priority service assistance for routine service problems, the program will fail and they and their customers will be the ultimate losers.

Finally, I think it is appropriate to remind your sales reps that if there were no problems there would be no need for a sales force. We fell down momentarily in the service area but we are taking steps to get back on top of it. During the interim period the sales reps will have to recognize valid service problems, learn to use the "hotline" system to greatest advantage to minimize customer dissatisfaction, and be confident in the knowledge that the situation is temporary and being corrected.

We remain open to any additional suggestions you or your salespeople may have. Let me know next Friday how your sales reps react to the service improvements which are coming and how well you feel they are using the "hotline" system.

Sincerely,

In response, a sales manager wrote this letter to his sales force.

Model Letter 6-6
(From the line sales manager to his sales force)

Dear _____:

The General Sales Manager has just informed me of   **(a)**
action being taken right now to improve speed and

quality of service. Additional service people and equipment are just part of the improvement. I'll describe all of the steps being taken when we get together on Monday morning.

We are also putting a procedure into effect to insure that no service problems occur which could give us a "black eye" in the market. Please review your accounts and identify any service problems which you consider crucial. Put the details of each situation in writing — keep it short — and be prepared to discuss them with me on Monday. I will describe a "hotline" system to insure customer satisfaction in crucial service situations when we meet.

We fell down momentarily in the service area but we *will* get back on top of it.

While the service improvements are being implemented, we have to recognize valid customer service problems when confronted with them, learn to use the new "hotline" system to greatest advantage, and be confident in the knowledge that this temporary situation is being corrected.

If you have any additional suggestions for keeping customers happy while the service department improvements are being implemented, I'd like to discuss them when we meet on Monday.

Sincerely,

Alternate Wording:

(a) You and I are very sensitive to the need for good service with our customers. I'm happy to tell you that the home office is just as sensitive to the need as we are. They too have sensed the recent slipping in the normally high quality of service we provide.

To remedy the problem they are expanding the size of the service department. They are also adding additional equipment so that service response time should be reduced considerably. I'll describe all the steps being taken when we get together on Monday morning.

3. ANNOUNCING CUTBACKS IN SERVICES

Management is sometimes faced with a choice of increasing prices or cutting back popular extra services. Particularly in times of inflation and rising costs, cutting back services may be chosen as a lesser evil than a price increase. This action is usually taken to keep the product competitive or, in other words, to help the sales force. However, the sales reps may not appreciate the "help" unless they can quickly see the advantage to them and their customers. These letters announcing cutbacks in service stress the positive benefits.

Model Letter 6-7
(From the chief sales officer to line sales managers)

Dear _____:

Material and labor costs have been rising rapidly in our industry. We have considered an across-the-board price increase. However, we feel an increase is undesirable at this time from a competitive stand-point.

The only alternative is to reduce costs. We are   **(a)** therefore eliminating the first service call which we previously provided the customer at no charge.

I believe your salespeople will prefer the elimination of the no-charge first service call to a price increase. Please communicate this policy to your sales force so they understand the advantage to them and to their customers.

Sincerely,

Alternate Wording:

(a) The only alternative is to reduce costs. Beginning November 1 we will no longer be able to provide the no-cost layout service as previously. Such a policy puts us in line with the remainder of the industry. A recent survey indicated we are the only company which provides this service at no charge. By eliminating the no-charge service, we can maintain our price and keep our salespeople in position to meet all competition.

Model Letter 6-8
(From line sales manager to his sales representatives)

Dear _____:

We've been wondering when the price increase would come. Well, we can stop wondering. The home office just informed me there will be no price increase! I think you'll agree this is the best news we've had in quite awhile.

Material and labor costs have been increasing and a **(a)** reduction of cost is necessary to enable us to hold the price. The first service call which we previously provided the customer at no charge has been eliminated. I think you'll agree it's a good deal.

I suggest you make a call on new customers approximately 30 days after delivery. If you feel minor adjustments are called for, you may wish to sell the customer on a service call. A little extra effort after the sale will pay dividends, so let's keep the customer happy and maintain our competitive price.

Sincerely,

Alternate Wording:

(a) Material and labor costs have been increasing, and a reduction of cost is necessary to enable us to hold the price. As a result, effective November 1, we will no longer offer a no-charge layout service as in the past. Although no-charge layout service has been an advantage we have all been able to use, I am sure you will agree that remaining competitive price-wise is a much greater advantage.

The price schedule for our layout service is attached. You will find it is very competitive with other companies offering a similar service.

Occasionally a service is no longer necessary or is no longer economically feasible and must be dropped. The communication should point out that the service is no longer needed and make it clear that its elimination should not affect sales.

Model Letter 6-9

Dear _____:

We have been informed by _____ Refrigeration Company that effective the end of next month they are discontinuing installation of air conditioners.

Most of our vehicles are now available with factory air conditioning. Many of you have already made local installation arrangements with air specialty shops or have trained people to do your own installations.

While initially the elimination of this service may cause some inconvenience, the need for it has become minimal and more practical alternatives have replaced it. Therefore, we are not planning to provide an installation service to replace _____ Refrigeration Company.

Some dealers who have a number of trained people may be interested in installing units for other dealers. If this is the case, please let me know and we will publish a listing of dealers who would be willing to provide such a service.

Sincerely,

7

LETTERS THAT IMPROVE SALES PERFORMANCE AND CHANGE BEHAVIOR

7

LETTERS THAT IMPROVE
SALES PERFORMANCE
AND CHANGE BEHAVIOR

Most sales managers feel one of the most rewarding parts of the job is watching salespeople develop and grow. The sales manager's part in the growth of his/her salesperson starts when he/she observes unacceptable performance. Actually, the sales management job calls for constantly observing and analyzing the performance of each individual in the sales force — the veterans as well as the rookies, the top producers as well as the lower third. The sales manager is responsible for correcting poor performance, taking positive action to help the salesperson become as productive as he or she can possibly be.

A sales manager once told me he fired his lowest two producers each year, even though the two lowest in his branch might be among the top 30% in the national sales force. My reaction was that if he had the kind of talent working for him that could produce that kind of result working for a judge, think what they could produce working for a coach. An effective sales manager in the face-to-face management of salespeople is a manager who actively causes people to grow. It's a lot like being an Olympic coach. If the athlete misses a dive, the coach points out specifically how to do it better next time. The coach doesn't berate the diver. A salesperson is motivated by the boss if the boss is competent and supportive in specific ways*.

Attempting to resolve a performance problem without first understanding the cause is like trying to put out a fire without knowing what type of material is burning. You can make conditions worse by applying the wrong solution. Correcting sales performance involves some manager sleuthing to determine why salespeople are behaving in an incorrect way. Do they know how to perform as you want them to? If they know how to do it "your way" but persist in using another method, why are they doing that? Answers to questions such as these will determine the type of corrective action which will be most successful. Determining the cause of performance problems is a subject in itself, the point is that the solution you provide must be tailored to the cause of the problem.

Some performance problems, by their nature, require face-to-face handling. For example, if a complex solution is required, such as coaching to handle a special type of sales approach, or if the problem is of a personal nature, personal handling is certainly in order. There remain many instances in which a letter is most efficient, timely, and economical. And even when a personal correction is required, a letter is desirable as a follow-up to fix points of agreement and to ensure that agreed-upon action is taken.

Both types of letters are provided in this section. Where personal contact is likely to be more effective, we have so indicated and have provided a follow-up letter that has proven effective in nailing down the points agreed upon in the meeting.

1. SUGGESTING MORE SALES CALLS

It happens to the best of your salespeople. They just stop making even the minimum number of sales calls it takes to produce satisfactory

---

* For specific suggestions on improving sales force productivity and a proven five-step method for coaching individual salespeople on sales calls, see the book *Successful Sales Management* by Hal Fahner; Prentice-Hall, Inc., 1983.

results. It's often a small thing that wakes you up to what's happening. Maybe you look over a weekly call report that so obviously reflects a goof-off week that you pull the previous month of reports and find little sales activity. There are times — hard times — when everybody knows nobody will buy until times get better — and most of your salespeople are making only a few calls, waiting for times to get better. Also, in summer the troops may get discouraged by the number of buyers/decision makers on vacation and some salespeople will make fewer sales calls.

Model Letter 7-1

Dear _____:

Today I sat down and compared June results with last June results. I looked first at units sold and dollar volume. Then I looked at the number of sales calls. You wouldn't believe it.

You made 15% fewer calls this June than you made last June, sold 21% fewer units, and your dollar volume declined 14% (inflation). I won't bother comparing your commission last June with this year because you must have already noticed that part.

There's a pattern there. You'll never guess what I **(a)** suggest we try. I suspect the summer slowdown among your prospects and customers has affected you. Well, you know that July and August is worse ("I can't see you for two weeks — vacation"). I suggest you spend two days at home phone-prospecting and get your appointment book up to Jan./Feb./Mar. levels — right now. I've charted last year's sales call activity and the number of calls I expect from you this July and August.

Notice that I'm expecting just two more calls a week this year than last. That's because it is tougher selling this year and it will take more effort — and I'd also like to see you get back the volume and income you gave up in June. You can get your sales and earnings back above last year.

Make the calls!

Sincerely,

Alternate Wording:

(a) This really got me curious, so I compared last April and May. Sure enough, you made 12% fewer calls this April and 14% less in May. If you continue this pattern of fewer calls each month, by October you'll never leave the house. Seriously, Al, we need to get back on track.

Model Letter 7-2

Dear _____:

You're always about a step ahead of me, so if I've noticed it you must be well aware of it, too. You are making fewer sales calls than normal, fewer than either of us would call even acceptable. Based on past experience, you can expect a drop in sales to follow.

I want you to continue the pace you have going so far   **(a)**
this year and I know you do too. Now is the time to look to the basics and keep the level of sales call activity where we know it must be to produce the volume you want. Why don't you develop a plan that includes bringing the number of calls up to the level of last year — and add a few to get back the ground you lost last month.

Send me your plan by next Friday and we'll discuss it   **(b)**
during our Friday phone call.

Sincerely,

Alternate Wording:

(a) I know you still plan to make the Paradise Island, Nassau trip. This sales activity level might get you as far as Cedar Point or Niagara Falls. I know you can do better.

(b) You just need to create a written plan and then work your plan. Some time each weekend jot down the names of prospects you plan to call on during the next week. Compare the number with the average you were maintaining in the first quarter when you were setting personal records. If the week plan doesn't equal or exceed your first quarter average, find more prospects.

Model Letter 7-3

Dear _____:

You know the old cliché — selling is like a funnel. You can't expect to get more out of the bottom than you put in the top.

Actually, in our business we can look at the company average and predict how much will come out the bottom of the funnel this month based on how much we put in the funnel last month:

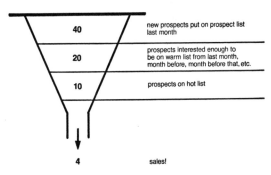

And you know as well as I do, anytime you let that top **(a)** number go below 40 new prospects in the funnel, the number of prospects on your Warm List will drop below 20. And when your Warm List gets down, your Hot List will drop below ten. And when your Hot List this month gets below ten, you know the only way you're going to get four sales this month is if you get lucky with a call-in — if out of the blue a prospect you've never heard of calls in and says, "Please, send somebody, just anybody out to take my order — the purchasing agent next door says you are the best."

Yes, the month can be saved by dumb luck. Seriously, I know you are a professional who respects the law of averages in this industry. So let's talk Friday. Be **(b)** prepared to tell me what you're doing to get your new prospect-call numbers back up to where they have to be.

Sincerely,

Alternate Wording:

(a) One sale requires about ten calls on new prospects (average). This fact is based on the experience of the entire sales force. The average sale is approximately $5,000. Using these figures, you can easily see how many new prospect calls per month you must average. See why I'm concerned?

(b) Would a step-up in sales effort be worthwhile? It could put you in position to win the salesperson of the year award. Let me know by the 15th how you plan to approach this opportunity to improve sales. I'm sure you can make it pay off.

Model Letter 7-4

Dear _____:

Have you noticed the red flag that's showing on your call reports? The flag is the definite slowing of the number of calls you are currently making as compared to last year. Based on past experience, a drop in volume will follow close behind.

I know you want to maintain the good sales record **(a)** you have going this year. Now is the time to look to the basics such as the number of calls you are making every day. Why don't you develop a plan right now that includes bringing the number of calls you make up to at least the level you were at last year.

Let's discuss your plan when we talk by phone Friday. **(b)**

Sincerely,

Alternate Wording:

(a) I know you plan on qualifying for the Acapulco trip. Now's the time to eliminate any potential sales problems that could stand in the way of that trip.

(b) Planning is a big part of the answer. Write down all of the prospects you know you're going to call on in the next month, whether you've contacted them for an appointment yet or not. If you don't have enough prospect names down on paper, you know you'll have trouble finding enough new prospects to call on later in the month — so put in extra prospecting work now. And then get into action selling appointments by phone and mail so you've got yourself a busy schedule of new prospect calls for the coming month.

2. SUGGESTING CALLS ON LARGER ACCOUNTS

Many salespeople have worked their way into mediocrity or even complete failure by concentrating their efforts on smaller, relatively unproductive accounts.

Why do they keep calling on the small accounts and neglect the important ones?

Well, because one can call on most small accounts with very little preparation. Smaller prospects aren't likely to brush you off. They are sometimes even flattered by attention from a larger supplier and will talk to this salesperson for hours even if they have no intention of buying. You don't have to deal with a buying committee or sell multiple buying influences. You'll usually get an order, although a small one, and that keeps the wolf from the door, the sales manager off your back.

Contrast that with the situation with large accounts where it's difficult to get in to see the buyer. They'll stand you up or cancel appointments on short notice because a meeting came up. You've got to sell multiple buying influences or buying committees as well as the main decision-maker. The decision-making process can drag on for months while the sales manager is on your back for results *now*, this month.

Why do they keep calling on just small accounts and neglect the important ones? Why should they call on key accounts? It's part of sales management's job to keep reminding even the best and most experienced salespeople to keep a balance in the class of accounts they call on and keep after the key accounts.

Model Letter 7-5

Dear _____:

We're not paying you what you're worth! I came to this conclusion while analyzing your sales production for the past few months. You were the number-one producer of new accounts in our District Office, and in the entire Eastern Region. However, you were twelfth in our District sales force of 15 and in the bottom quartile in the Region in dollar volume. Talk about good news/bad news!

I also took a good look at your territory. You do not **(a)** have a larger number of small businesses in your territory than others in the District. If anything, your territory is heavier in large accounts than our other territories.

You have proven your sales ability and I'm happy to have the large number of new accounts you've produced so far this year. I see the situation described above as an opportunity, certainly not a problem. The same talents you have demonstrated in increasing new accounts will serve you well in bringing in the largest prospects. Surprisingly, the larger account often requires about the same number of calls as the smaller account. Some of the "homework" and methods differ slightly, but I suspect you'll be able to adjust quickly.

Let's discuss it Monday and make plans to make calls together the following week. I'm eager to see your volume up with your unit sales production, and your commissions up where you deserve for the amount of hard work you are putting in.

Sincerely,

Alternate Wording:

(a) By the way, if you had sold the same number of accounts equally divided between Class A (large), B (middle), and C (small) classification accounts, you would be in the *top 15%* of the entire sales force nationwide!

Model Letter 7-6

Dear _____:

If we were filling a dump truck with sand and you had your choice of using a spade or a bulldozer, which would you use? In your sales territory the larger the account, the quicker the quota is reached and surpassed and the greater the earnings. Although the large volume account may be harder to land, the returns make it a highly profitable venture. Here's an example. In a study the company conducted recently,   **(a)**
we learned that the $5,000 per year account requires about 40 hours per year to sell and service. The $50,000 account requires about 100 hours per year. That makes each hour spent on the larger account 400% more profitable. You don't have to be a Harvard Ph.D. to figure out how you can increase

your income. I'm suggesting you concentrate on prospects and customers with $30,000 per year annual volume potential or more. That doesn't mean abandoning the smaller accounts you have now. Just concentrate on the larger prospects as you sell new accounts. The net result to you will be more sales, larger commissions, and an easier sales job. I believe you will also find it more interesting since large accounts tend to have more variety and more interesting problems to solve with our products.

Sincerely,

Alternate Wording:

(a) Doesn't it stand to reason that selling the larger accounts requires about the same number of calls as selling the small accounts? Granted, you may have to make an extra call or two and sell to a second buying influence. You may have to sell "smarter," do a little extra homework on a large one sometimes. On the other hand, the smaller account may have to squeeze more out of every dollar and be more demanding, actually require more proof and sales effort.

Here is a model letter for the salesperson who is more comfortable calling on smaller accounts even though aware of the more profitable larger account.

Model Letter 7-7

Dear _____:

Here's a firm offer for an extra $200 for the first account you land that buys over 16,000 units per year. Why am I willing to pay such a bonus? Well, for one thing the larger account is worth more to the company, but, even more important at this point, I wish to give you incentive to go after the larger account.

We've talked about this before. Since our last discussion I have been reviewing all the possible reasons other salepeople I have worked with have given for not calling on larger accounts. Here are the major ones:

1. Selling larger companies requires meeting with committees.

2. Locating the real decision-maker/buyer is difficult.

3. You are often dealing with a specialist in a big company, and they can be very demanding for detailed technical information.

4. You usually have invested a lot of time and effort by the time a big deal goes sour. Missing on a smaller prospect doesn't cost you as much.

5. I know the small accounts, how they think, how to approach them. I have a proven track record there.

Recognize any of the above reasons? As we have discussed in the past, every salesperson must get a balance of accounts. You can't afford to spend all your time on small prospects and customers.

You run out of time before your dollar volume reaches the neccesary level when you call on nothing but small accounts. Staying with just small accounts will limit your sales success, your earnings, and even your future with this company.

Here's a little homework that will help both you and   **(a)**
me. Take a few minutes to write out why each of the reasons for not selling large accounts is a fallacy. Send me your written thoughts by next Tuesday. We can discuss them by telephone.

Here's to that first $16,000-per-year account.

Sincerely,

Alternate Wording:

(a) At our sales meeting next Monday we are going to discuss the fallacy behind each of these reasons to sell only small accounts. Please be prepared to take about five minutes to discuss points three and four. Some of the others are doing the same with the other points.

3. REQUESTING IMPROVEMENT IN PAPERWORK

The good news is that salespeople don't all hate paperwork as much as most sales managers think they do. The bad news is that some salespeople do hate paperwork that much.

It is important to make performance matter. If the sales manager isn't consistent in demanding timely reporting from the sales staff, they won't report. Sales managers who have been successful in getting reports submitted when due have found the solution lies with emphasizing how the salesperson benefits. So, make it matter, keep reminding them of deadlines, and remind the salespeople of the benefit to them.

Here's a letter that uses the direct approach.

Model Letter 7-8

Dear _____:

I'm embarrassed! I have to admit I've been neglecting my paperwork. But today I dug in and got caught up. And you'll never guess what I discovered while I was getting caught up — you've been neglecting your paperwork! You haven't sent in a call report in three weeks. And you got away with it because I had gotten behind, too. Well, the party's over. Since I've reformed, you're going to have to shape up.

You must be completing the reports for your own use even if you haven't sent them in, because they are valuable to you. Call reports must be completed immediately after a call to enable you to capture everything you learned and also to insure that you'll be ready to plan the next call effectively and move forward to the sale. You can't keep track of your hot list, much less your warm list, if you neglect call reports. So, I know you've been filling them out. Send them in!

Sincerely,

Model Letter 7-9

Dear _____:

Yes, Sales Call Reports are important to me and this office for recordkeeping. But that is not the major reason for completing and turning them in regularly.

The real reasons are those that are important to you. Other salespeople have told me that their call reports are worth up to $5,000 per year in additional income to them. Here's why.

The Sales Call Report is your memory. It enables you to capture what you know about your prospect's situation and helps you prepare for the next call. Your Call Reports are your hot list and therefore your savings account.

The Sales Call Report provides the means for planning your sales activities. It reduces wasted calls, helps you to reduce unnecessary driving, helps you pinpoint exactly what you intend to accomplish on each call. A sustained record of your calls helps you determine if you are making enough of each type of call and where to increase your emphasis. When I analyze your call reports each week I can be of help to you if you are slightly off target on balance of calls or type of prospect, for instance. Sometimes someone else can see things from the outside that you are too close to and can't see yourself. I can also benefit from trends or things happening in the market that you spot and pass on to me. I can relay these tips to the rest of the salespeople — and, in the same way, transmit their helpful hints to you.

So complete your Call Reports every day and send them in every Friday. It's worth $5,000 per year to you.

Sincerely,

Model Letter 7-10

Dear _____:

I've been putting together a mailing to prospects based on sales calls made last quarter. I was rolling right along until I hit your territory. Either you took a vacation last quarter or you just took a vacation from turning in call reports. Since you were second highest in sales last quarter, you either sold every prospect you called on or never turned in reports unless you made the sale.

It's embarrassing to me that I didn't jump on you at the time. I promise it won't happen again. You'll hear from me immediately if you don't get your reports in on time in the future. The importance really hit me when I couldn't get this mailing out for your territory. I'm sure this direct mail will stimulate warm leads and result in increased sales.

Go back over your records for the last quarter. I'll talk to you next Monday and see if we can salvage some direct mail support for you.

Sincerely,

4. PREPARING FOR COACHING CALLS

No sales management responsibility is more important than coaching. When the sales manager has been making coaching calls on a regular basis, a trusting relationship develops and salespeople are willing to open up and tell the manager where they are having problems — that they think they are losing sales because they can't handle objections, for instance. The salespeople come to see the boss as a source of help, who is capable of teaching them and building their sales skill.

However, salespeople are likely to view their first coaching experience with suspicion and fear — especially veterans who may have worked for managers in the past who made calls with the attitude of a judge, who was out in the field to find out if any of the sales force was worth keeping or if they should all be fired. So is it surprising that the salesperson's reaction may be to keep the boss from finding out what is really going on in the territory? That the salesperson tries to take the manager to those accounts where little opportunity for coaching exists? The salesperson may feel that if they have problems with opening, objection handling, closing, they have to work it out for themselves. How does a sales manager get past this barrier and develop a healthy coaching relationship with each salesperson?

Successful coaching depends on proper groundwork. You can prepare your salesperson for an area of concentration prior to your visit. For example, you may strongly suspect too few calls are being made on new accounts based on call reports. You decide to concentrate on first calls with your salesperson. A phone conversation and a letter could be used to pave the way for a first-call coaching session.

Model Letter 7-11

Dear _____:

I look forward to working with you on September 8th and 9th. I do appreciate you meeting me at Syracuse airport the evening of September 7th. If you don't mind a late supper, we can go over the calls for the next day while we grab a bite that night.

As we discussed, we haven't added many new accounts in the last six months. We will be concentrating on first calls during our two days together. We'll look for additional ways of prospecting, preparing for the first call, and methods and sales tools to use on the first call.

See you September 7th. Keep selling!

Sincerely,

Model Letter 7-12

Dear _____:

My plans call for meeting with you on Monday and Tuesday of next week. I would like to ride with you as you make your regular calls on accounts. Don't plan anything out of the ordinary. Just make those calls you would regularly make on those days.

We should both benefit from making these calls together. I may be able to pick up sales tips others in the region can use. In turn, I may be able to pass on some ideas to you that others have found valuable.

Although I'll accompany you on every call, I will not be entering into the sale itself. Then, after the call, we can discuss some of the things that happened and why.

Based on the reactions of other salespeople who have already been involved in this experience, I believe you will find it rewarding. Other salespeople have told me:

1. They have picked up new sales approaches. For example, Bill Anderson was able to find

an answer to an objection which caused considerable difficulty in the past.

2. They have been able to get a fresh approach to a particularly difficult prospect. I won't join in to help you sell a tough customer, but I can give you an unbiased and fresh insight into the problem. That has happened recently on three occasions.

3. They have been able to identify problem areas that previously escaped them. We can be so close to a problem that we can't see an obvious solution.

I am looking forward to meeting with you Monday. I'll see you in your office at 8:30 a.m. ready for a busy day.

Sincerely,

5. COUNSELING IN AREAS AFFECTING JOB PERFORMANCE

Everything we have discussed regarding improving sales performance and changing behavior so far has been clearly sales-skill-related. But we know that occurences in their personal lives sometimes affect on-the-job behavior and performance. What should a sales manager do? First, realize that you are in a sensitive area when the employee's personal life overlaps with the job — for example: money problems, suspected alcohol or chemical dependency, frequent absence, spending time on outside interests, "moonlighting" on another job.

Second, get clear on your company policy before the fact — don't wait until the situation occurs. If you are a large organization, sit down with personnel or industrial relations and go over the parameters for dealing with these situations. If you are a small company, sit down with the company's attorney and discuss these potential situations and get guidelines to follow. The price of a couple of hours of your attorney's time is small compared to the alternative.

Third, recognize that you do have rights as an employer to correct or dismiss on the basis of unacceptable job performance which may have happened to result from occurences in the salesperson's personal life. For example, everyone knows Charlie lives in a bottle all weekend. But for the last six weeks he hasn't made calls on Monday or Tuesday and his sales were down 40% last quarter compared to last year. We are not officially concerned about Charlie leaving the planet on his own time, Saturday and Sunday. Rather, we obviously have every right to expect acceptable performance on Monday. We may insist our employee's behavior conform to company standards. We may counsel him or her to change unacceptable on-the-job behavior. This would include suggesting they seek help to correct, for instance, a drinking problem so that they can raise their on-the-job performance back to acceptable level.

Fourth, words on paper definitely commit the company. Get guidance from personnel or legal whenever you suspect you are in a gray area. The following letters are general and can be modified to fit your company policy.

Addressing a Drinking Problem

Chemical abuse and/or drinking often causes loss of time on the job, poor customer relations, and reduced volume. The problem is so widespread that most sales managers have faced it at least once. Because of the addictive nature of the problem, the employee will often promise to make corrections and then fall back into the problem. This letter encourages the salesperson to take the action promised by putting the agreement in writing.

Model Letter 7-13

Dear _____:

I want to thank you for the frankness with which you discussed your drinking pattern at our meeting.

To recall some of the main points of our discussion:

1. Drinking to excess creates job problems. Among the more important is time lost on the job. You indicated that you have lost several days in the past couple of months because of alcohol intake. Driving constitutes a second problem. Driving from one account to another with even a small amount of alcohol intake constitutes an increased risk —for you, for others on the road, and for the company. You indicated that on occasion you have been drinking while on the job. The third problem is the effect your drinking has on your job performance and the customers you serve. Alcohol dulls the senses and cripples your work efficiency. Not only are

your job decisions second best, but your customers undoubtedly sense they are not getting the service and care they deserve.

2. You acknowledge the problem and promise **(a)** to combat it. Your first step is to contact a member of Alcoholics Anonymous to join that organization. I have provided you with the name and telephone number of a local member.

3. I have agreed that you will continue in your **(b)** present position on the condition that you join the Alcoholics Anonymous group and follow their instructions, and you again comply with company work standards as a result.

This is an important crossroad. The decisions and action you take in the next several weeks will determine your future. Many others have faced this problem and won. You can too. I'm pulling for you and know you can do it. Let me know in a few days what progress you have made.

Sincerely,

Alternate Wording:

(a) You acknowledge that you have something of an alcohol problem but you feel you can handle it without outside assistance. You have promised you will not drink while on the job and that you will not permit alcohol to interfere with the performance of your work. I have made it clear that you must improve your job performance.

(b) I have agreed that you may continue in your present position. However, we agree that we will meet weekly to review your progress in handling this problem. Any indication that this problem is persisting will require more stringent solutions.

Correcting Pursuit of Outside Interests on Company Time

Salespeople are often gregarious types and usually have a high energy level. They often are "joiners" and may become active in the organizations they affiliate with. If this overlaps into the sales job and affects performance, we may have to supply the discipline the salesperson lacks.

Model Letter 7-14

Dear _____:

Here's a way to say "no" in three languages:

"nyet"   "non"   "nein"

I learned them from our company treasurer. He knows how to say "no" in 101 languages.

At some time or other we all find it difficult to say no. But sometimes it's necessary. Take clubs for instance. If you said yes to every club or office offered, there would be no time for anything else. And that brings me to my point. I don't know of every club and office you take part in, but I know you invest a good deal of time. And that's fine when it's on your time and recreational. And, yes, I realize some of it is good for contacts and related to your sales. And I know you will agree that the time and effort invested is far in excess of the sales benefits. All I ask is that you answer these questions with your characteristic openness and honesty. Have you been finding yourself at luncheons that drag on into the afternoon? Have you found it necessary to take care of association business during working hours? Have you found that club affairs were creeping into your thoughts when you should be concerned with business? Are any of these things related to the recent decrease in your sales and drop from our perennial top sales producer in the Region down into the middle of the pack? All of these are symptoms of the need to say "no" more frequently.

If any of these symptoms fit your situation, learn at least these three ways to say "no." I can provide more if needed.

Sincerely,

Questioning Frequent Absence/Sickness

The salesperson who misses work often because of reported illness can be a delicate problem. The problem is that the possibilities range from a legitimate health problem which could be serious with this frequency of being too ill to work, all the way across the spectrum to looking for another job or chemical dependency.

The first step is to provide the salesperson an opportunity to explain excessive absences. Many sales managers handle this step by phone, seeking an explanation by letter only after the salesperson has been absent from work many times. When it is used is a matter of management preference.

Model Letter 7-15

Dear _____:

I'm sure nothing upsets you more than having to miss a day of work. Most of us feel that we are in some way shirking our responsibility. This concern makes a legitmate illness all the more difficult to bear. Your call reports indicate that you have been ill on three different occasions each of the past two months. A record of illness such as this is certainly beyond the ordinary. I know it must be of concern to you. Your absence is also of concern to me. In the first place I want to be of assistance to you or your family should you be encountering some difficulty. Second, your illness represents a significant loss to the company in sales and in customer good will.

Can I be of assistance? **(a)**

Sincerely,

Alternate Wording:

(a) If you have not had a physical to determine the nature of your problem, I would strongly urge you to do so. In the meantime, can I be of any help to you and your family?

Correcting the Moonlighting Sales Representative

The personal freedom that is built into the sales job requires self-discipline from sales professionals. Salespeople generally come and go on their own schedule to a great degree, and we hold them responsible for number of calls and amount of sales, not for being at an office. Salespeople have the opportunity to engage in outside activities. Some sales reps may try selling a sideline product along with the primary employer's product. Most sales organizations have an uncompromising company policy against this practice, often providing for instant dismissal and often stated in strong language that comes close to, "Hey, you wanna be an independent agent selling every available product? Then hang out your mfg. rep. shingle and do it. But not on a base/draw from us. Goodbye!"

Sometimes a rep will take a part-time evening job totally unrelated to the sales job. Although less obviously a conflict of interest, the moonlighting activity will detract energy from the sales job. The real problem in both instances is a salesperson not totally engrossed in maximizing sales of the employer's product and not making sufficient commissions or seeing the realistic possibility of substantial earnings for more sales effort. Showing the sales force the opportunity with our product and company and getting them to maximize their efforts does sound like sales management's job.

Model Letter 7-16

Dear _____:

As you may be learning, selling for _____ is more than a full-time job. Experience has taught us, and may already have taught you, too, that it is impossible to sell two lines at the same time.

I am referring to your present efforts to sell _____ products as well as ours. Here are just two difficulties you will encounter:

1. You will not have time to represent each line effectively. Selling a second line requires added time for locating and qualifying prospects, making an explanation of the line to the prospect, servicing, setting up displays, handling complaints and problems. Clearly, your position with _____ Co. requires your full time, and added activities detract from the performance of your job.

2. Any problems you have with your sideline —supply, quality, service — will have a negative impact on our products, our reputation, our company. Our customers do not make a clear distinction between our products and others you may handle. Problems with the sideline become associated with our product.

You can easily see why it is our company policy that **(a)** no _____ Co. sales representative carry any other line in addition to ours. Also, I can assure you on the basis of many years of observation of this industry that you will make more money selling our product line exclusively than by representing any combination of products.

Our company policy is clear. The company permits no exceptions to this policy. To do so would lead to problems and limited sales effectiveness. Let me know by Friday what you intend to do about your second line

Sincerely,

Alternate Wording:

(a) In the interest of the company and our customers, no one is permitted to carry a second line of products. If this leads to some complication of which I am unaware, let me know. Otherwise I will expect you to drop the second line immediately.

Model Letter 7-17

Dear _____:

I received a request in my morning mail indicating **(a)** you are considering a part-time job working evenings, Saturday, and Sunday in addition to your sales career with _____ Co.

I was surprised, and frankly my initial reaction was that I had failed you. Part of my sales management job is to make clear to you the scope of the opportunity you have as a sales representative for _____ Co. — that you have a career with us, not just an 8 to 5 job.

The opportunity is not just long-term, that some day you will be a manager. Rather, you also have a right-now opportunity to make commissions that make the money you would make at this part-time evening and weekend job look insignificant.

I just pulled your sales record for the last couple of months. Respectable, not bad for a rep with less than six months experience. However, I've seen enough the few times we've made calls together to know you can increase your volume substantially. If you put the same energy, time, and effort into your sales career here that you would have to put into this part-time venture, the immediate return in earnings will be three times what the part-time earnings would have been. And the career growth and action of the sales activity compared to a clerking job — no comparison. If you put in the extra energy and time — I will, too. Give your sales career the extra time instead of the part-time job and I'll work with you two days a week for the next 60 days. We'll get you five years experience in two months. Although other salespeople have attempted part-time work, few of them were successful. The decision is yours to make. **(b)** And as you consider this important juncture in your career, I hope you will consider my advice.

Let me know your decision by the end of the week.

Sincerely,

Alternate Wording:

(a) You mentioned the other day that you had taken a part-time job to help pay some extra bills that have piled up. I can understand the economic pressure that brought you to such a decision.

(b) The decision is yours to make. In reaching the right decision, you must compare the certainty of the small amount of guaranteed immediate cash with the long-term advantage of career growth and possible, but not guaranteed, substantial additional current earnings.

8

MEMORANDUMS TO MANAGEMENT AND STAFF PERSONNEL

8

MEMORANDUMS
TO MANAGEMENT
AND STAFF PERSONNEL

MEMO

TO: Readers of Sales

FROM: Hal Fahner & Morris Miller

SUBJECT: Origin of Memos & Purpose of Memos

The purpose of this memo is:

1. To point out the uses and limitations of the communication device commonly known as the "Memo."

2. To convince you of the importance of following the ten basic rules of memo-writing which appear in Chapter 8 of this book.

The memorandum is an old and useful communication device. The first written reference to a "memorand" appeared in 1433 in the Rolls of Parliament in England. In 1465, a written communication to Thomas More began "Memorandum to Thomas More that because ye myzt foryete myne errand to Maister Bernay, I pray you rede hym my bille." The terminology caught on and ever since we've been sending each other memos. The device evolved to become a common business tool described as follows in the *Oxford English Dictionary*:

An informal epistolary communication, without signature or formulae of address or subscription, usually written on paper with a printed heading bearing the word "Memorandum" and the name and address of the sender.

The memo pinpoints a specific area and requests action. It provides a written record of the request for action to both the sender and receiver. It enables the writer to convey a sense of urgency that action take place. Properly used, the memo can be a powerful tool for the sales manager. Misused, it has ended promising careers.

There are some common-sense rules you can follow which will save you from the lethal dangers of bad memos. Refer to the ten Basic Rules in this chapter for a month or your next 50 memos (or whichever comes first), and always open this book and review the rules when writing an important and very visible memo. You cannot afford to skim this chapter. Please read it carefully.

THE TEN BASIC RULES OF MEMOS

If we followed our own rules in writing the memo above, you should be eager to know the ten rules we referred to and how you can use memos to get action.

Here are the ten Basic Rules of Memos:

1. *The Message Comes First.* Put the most important information first, at the very beginning of your memo. Get to the point fast. Start with the conclusion and use the rest of the memo to convince the reader, supporting the conclusion.

2. *Tell the Reader What You Want Done.* Clearly ask for the action you want. A memo should leave no doubt in the mind of the receiver about what the writer wants done.

3. *Use Simple Language.* People generally tend to become much more formal when they put words on paper than when they speak. The result is often that we sound pompous on paper. Write like you talk. Keep a conversational tone. Read it back to yourself. Ask yourself if that's how you'd say it if you were face-to-face.

4. *Use Short, Simple Sentences.* Avoid long sentences. Use less than 20 words per sentence. You'll probably average 15 to 20 words per sentence. Put only one thought in a sentence.

5. *Use a Dictionary.* Also utilize a thesaurus and check grammar and spelling. Proofread everything. Train your secretary to be extra-careful in these areas in your memos. If you travel a lot, your secretary can make you look illiterate and sloppy — or like top-management material.

6. *Observe the Appropriate Chain of Command and Protocol.* Carbon copies, the "cc list," properly used helps insure action and complete communication. Proper use of the cc will also help gain you the respect and trust of your superiors, subordinates, and peers. Why do people who would never think of bypassing their boss and their boss' boss and talking directly to the Sr. VP or President think it's okay to use the cc list to do the same thing? Memos from clerks to supervisors but with cc's to 20 people from janitor level to VP are common.

   Also your secretary may be offending half the company for you by putting the folks on the cc list in order of importance. Use alphabetical order and you'll offend no one.

7. *Don't Use Memos as a Political Tool.* The ultimate memo mistake is to use the memo (and the cc list) as a tool to criticize another person or department. We've all seen feuds go public within a company through subtle reference in memos.

   When memos get nasty and cc lists expand attempting to recruit allies to each side, observers in the company often call them "machine gun memos." Well, he or she who lives by the machine gun memo will die by it eventually. They alienate many, and someone they've alienated will get them. If someone shoots at you with a memo, they are shooting themselves in the foot. Never shoot back.

8. *Use One Page or Less.* Some people become infamous throughout the company for memos with "thud value," 10 or 15 pages long.

   "Hey, did you receive your copy of Charlie's latest attempt at a best seller novel in the form of a memo? If you already read it, can you do me a favor and summarize it. What does he want us to do?"

   People will read a memo of one page or less. They'll understand it. They'll do what you request. You'll be very popular.

The greatest cause of thick memos is the mistake of attempting to include large amounts of technical information, back-up data, in the body of the memo. A more effective method is to attach the back-up data and refer to it in the one-page memo.

9. *Humor Can Be Dangerous.* Humor is never easy to use in business communication. There is the risk of being misunderstood, the meaning of the joke being misinterpreted. At least when we use humor in a business letter, we have just one reader interpreting our meaning. Memos often are sent to several main recipients (our six district managers, for example) and cc'd to others who may be affected or have a need to know (perhaps the advertising manager or credit manager). So the humor in a memo often must be interpreted in the same way by many individuals with different backgrounds and points of view. The joke better not be too subtle or controversial. Keep it simple.

10. *Use the Simplest Communication Method to Get the Job Done.* Sometimes a walk to the office down the hall is more appropriate and effective than a memo. Remember, an advantage of the memo over a conversation is the memo provides a written record of the request for action and enables the writer to convey a sense of urgency.

Sometimes a verbal agreement on a course of action between two departments is concluded by one department head saying to the other "Okay, let's do it that way. Send me a memo summarizing what we've agreed to. As soon as I read it and am sure we're both clear on every point we'll go ahead. And if we're off base with each other on any point, I'm sure we can get together and clear it up." Now that's obviously using what memos do best, clarifying and formalizing an interdepartment agreement and making it easy for every team member to do his or her proper part on a project. However, if we always use a memo first and talk later, our peers may feel we try to pressure them to do things our way by overusing the formal communication of a memo (see "machine gun memo"). There is a place for informal two-way verbal communication.

1. MEMOS TO THE SALES MANAGER'S MANAGER

Constant communication is one of the cornerstones of a good relationship with your boss. You hate surprises, your boss hates surprises. Keep the boss up-to-date about what is going on.

Memos to Keep the Manager Apprised

Model Memo 8-1

TO: Central Region Manager

FROM: Sales Manager, District 14

SUBJECT: Target Account Project

The purpose of this note is to bring you some good news about the target account project we started in District 14 three months ago. You authorized a $2,000 expenditure from my district budget to use an outside telemarketing specialist to follow up on target accounts after I did a mailing to them.

We agreed ten new accounts of the $100,000-per-year volume class in the next year from that mail-and-phone project would be great, and if we got that result we should do it on a larger scale next year. Well, in the first 90 days we've gotten first orders from four and second orders from three other target companies as a result of that project. The average order size has been approximately $10,000. The sales force is enthusiastic; I've never seen them so excited about sales potential. We are definitely on to something here. I want to discuss the possibility of expanding the project when we get together next week for our quarterly progress review.

Memos Requesting the Manager's Assistance

Sometimes we need help from our boss or the home office. An organized statement of the situation and a specific request for aid is most effective and appropriate.

Model Memo 8-2

TO: Central Region Manager

FROM: Sales Manager, District 12

SUBJECT: Competitive Activity

I want you to know about some unusual competitive activity in District 12. For years, the manufacturer's rep for Ajax Products has called on many of the same accounts we have served for years. There has never been any direct competition because their product line is complementary to ours, and the few items they do duplicate are light-duty and appeal to a different type of manufacturer than those that make up the bulk of our account list.

In the past six weeks, four of my six salespeople have lost small orders to the Ajax rep. The items involved are similar in design and quality to our own. And the price has been *15 to 20%* lower than ours.

Can you find out if any other districts have run into the same thing? Does headquarters know of a change in Ajax marketing? Can we expect this direct competition on a regular basis? Can they maintain the low prices or is this a temporary introductory price? In short, can you tell me what's going on? I've ordered my salespeople to get us Ajax price sheets and product samples and gather all information they can from the purchasing agents who have bought the new Ajax products. I will have a written report for you at our quarterly report meeting.

Memos Requesting Change

Model Memo 8-3

TO: Central Region Manager
FROM: Sales Manager, District 10
SUBJECT: Weekly Reports

I'm writing to request a change in the procedure for submitting reports to the Regional Office. As we discussed at the last regional meeting, all of the districts are having a difficult job getting weekly reports in on time. We get the weekly report from our salespeople on Monday. We review and file those reports and use that information to write our report to you. What often actually happens is a crisis arises Monday or Tuesday that we must deal with. When that happens, even with buring the midnight oil, we usually get the report to the region out on Thursday or Friday. And I think all of the district managers will admit that the quality of their report suffers. What I propose is giving us until close of business Friday afternoon to put the report in the mail to you. This would improve the quality of the reports you receive and allow the district managers more flexibility in dealing with crises. If you would like to try this schedule with just a couple of districts on a test basis to see how it works, I volunteer to be one of the test districts. What do you think?

Memos to Inform of New Sales Opportunity and Request Action or Authority

Sometimes an opportunity for increased sales looks so good that a sales manager wants to get on it right now. No waiting for headquarters to decide it's a good idea and do it companywide. Right now is the time in my territory, strike while the iron is hot. Well, sell the boss on the idea.

Model Memo 8-4

TO: Vice President, Sales

FROM: Central Region Manager

SUBJECT: Sales Promotion Project

We have an opportunity in the central region to get the new Model XX off to a flying start. I'm writing to ask your approval to go ahead with a sales promotion with all of the dealers in the region. My proposal will use up more than half of the total region advertising/promotion budget for the year. But the sales will justify the expenditure.

One of Mike Shumate's dealers in District 8 asked Mike if he would organize a promotion among all of the dealers in the district to hold a drawing for a new model XX. The dealers would do plenty of advertising, much of it under our co-op program, and promote the drawing. And, of course, that means advertising and promoting the model XX. The dealers in Mike's district all went for it because it was a dealer's idea and because it's a good idea. The dealers will buy the model XX to give away but they want Mike to come in for 1/6 from the district ad budget.

Well, you know how dealers keep in touch, so next thing Ted Johnson's dealers in District #9 come to him wanting the same deal as the District 8 dealers, and I hadn't approved Shumate's request yet. And, of course, today both Dick Klahr and Jim Hecht called. Their dealers have talked to dealers in Districts 8 and 9 and want the same deal. So, now the dealers in Districts 8, 9, 10, and 11 — the whole central region — want to use the same promotion for the new model XX. Since we were worried about how to get them to spend co-op ad money on the new model and they are now eager to do that, I'm saying let's let them do it!

To make this work, I need to authorize each of my four district managers to use part of their district advertising budget to go in with their dealers to buy a model XX for the drawing in their district. This will use up more than half of the annual ad/promo budget for the region for the year. But the dealers will be promoting and advertising the model XX all summer. And they'll be 100% behind this new product and giving it their best sales effort. I believe the sales results will be record-breaking.

I request permission to authorize each of my district managers to go ahead with this promotion.

2. MEMOS TO THE ADVERTISING DEPARTMENT

Staff people can be a great help to a sales manager. The Advertising Department can be particularly helpful. You can multiply the effectiveness of each of your salespeople with advertising backup. Work with them and ask for specific help, thank them, and praise them when they come through for you.

Model Memo 8-5

TO: Advertising Manager

FROM: District Sales Manager

SUBJECT: Help on Local TV Advertising

I need your help! The people who televise the state high school basketball tournament contacted me and I think it could be very effective for us. I've bounced it off my two best dealers and they're all for it. The rest of the dealers will fall in line if those two tell them it's a good deal.

But we need professional help. I suspect our agreement with the ad agency covers them buying such time to get their percentage as well. But beyond that, we need you to put together some sort of special promotion or sale to feature in our ads, adapt or customize a couple of the national spots to fit this, etc. And they are hitting me with the highest rates for coverage in Milwaukee, where I don't have a dealer right now. And they say they won't break it up, you pay for the whole state, or you're out. I suspect they have some room for compromise. They also have some requirements that we also take a few 30-second spots for the state girls basketball tournament and the swimming championships. They've got it all in a package. Anyway, I'm over my head and I need your expertise. I'm sure you can negotiate the best deal for us. And explain the co-op deal to any dealers who are unsure.

Will you jump in and coordinate a promo/sale and advertising package and present it to my dealers? I know this can be a big volume-producer for the district with your professional approach.

Sometimes the staff guys get a program going that causes some problems in the field. You're sure it seemed good when they looked at "the big picture," but it ain't working in Peoria. Tell them tactfully.

Model Memo 8-6

TO: Advertising Manager

FROM: District Sales Manager

SUBJECT: Products Emphasized in Advertising

My salespeople and I think the new advertising is very creative and well done. Our district is a little different than our neighboring districts, however. We've got some concerns we need your help on.

The last six weeks we've seen a lot of emphasis on skylights in the national ads. The ad mats we received feature a lot of these products. Our area is beginning to see "suburban sprawl" and perhaps our dealers will see a demand in a couple of years. However, right now most of our coverage is in markets that must be called rural rather than suburban. The dealers do a great job moving windows and doors. We have tried and just can't get them to promote products they consider different. The harsh climate and short summer are factors they cite in staying with traditional replacement products. And the rural regard for utility and distrust of fancy and exotic new products, which is how the dealers view the skylight line, are the reasons they give for staying with the basic products.

The dealers want advertising that sticks to the basic product. They feel they're losing part of the advantage our advertising can give them when a portion of the ad pushes products they don't believe apply to their market.

Please respond quickly or come out and see for yourself. We've got to either convince the dealers to be satisfied with the ads as they are running now or change the ads run in this district. We must react within ten days to two weeks or they'll be dissatisfied with anything we do. Please respond quickly. Thanks for your help.

Memos to Show Appreciation for a Problem Well-Handled

When the staff people come through, thank them. And let your boss know and their boss know how much they helped. Also, make sure they know that you let everyone else know how well they did. Do this and they'll be there any time you need them.

Model Memo 8-7

TO: Advertising Manager

FROM: District Sales Manager

SUBJECT: Current Season Product Advertising

Thank you for your fast, effective response to my request for help. I never expected the magic you worked in the meeting with district salespeople and dealers.

Thanks to your skillful handling of the discussion, the dealers are open to some attempts to sell new products. And they are very pleased by your understanding of their position and modification of ads to emphasize the standard product line.

I've never seen the dealers more enthused at the support they get from our company. All of us in District 10 thank you for your prompt, effective action. And the District 10 sales force and I want you to know we've never seen anyone handle dealers more skillfully. Our hats are off to you — you are a master salesperson, and that is our highest compliment!

cc: Central Region Manager
    Director, Marketing Services
    District 10 Sales Force

Model Memo 8-8

TO: Advertising Manager

FROM: District Sales Manager

SUBJECT: Local TV Advertising — Thank You!

Have you seen the sales figures for District 10 for last month? It's a new record for that time period. And the current month is also far ahead of last year. The dealers are still working as fast as they can on the backlog of sales leads generated by the high school basketball tournament TV advertising. Your work in convincing the most conservative dealers to spend a little more, the promo and sale package you created, the modified commercials, and the great deal you negotiated for us made the record sales month possible. District 10 could not have put this project together without you. Thank you for your hard work and creativity. You deserve the lion's share of the credit for the record sales. Thanks again, from the entire District 10 organization.

CC: Central Region Manager
    Director, Marketing Services
    District 10 Sales Force

3. MEMOS TO THE SERVICE DEPARTMENT

The interdependence of the Sales and Service Departments demands close communication and understanding between them. If product is not sold there is no need for a Service Department. But more important, poor service results in lost sales. On the other side of the coin, an excellent service program provides an important value that can be sold along with other product features.

A good relationship between sales manager and service manager is a must. On many occasions a personal visit or telephone call will keep communication channels open. Sometimes the subject of the communication will require written memos to provide a record of the conversation or a quick memo may be a simpler device than a personal visit or telephone call.

Keep in mind that positive memos expressing encouragement and commendation are just as important as those exploring problems. The first memos included here are those exploring difficulties. The last explores commendations.

Model Memo 8-9

TO: Service Manager

FROM: Sales Manager

SUBJECT: Priestly Company

As discussed, the Priestly Company should warrant a special service representative. That representative would devote a minimum of 50% of his or her time to that account. The service rep would identify problems, perform service as requested by Priestly Co., and act as liaison with our company to arrange more complex service as required. This we both feel will resolve the service problem reported by Priestly Company and will maintain this important account.

Thanks, Bill, for your assistance.

Model Memo 8-10

TO: Service Manager

FROM: Sales Manager

SUBJECT: Handling Troubled Service Problems

URGENT

You and I are well aware chronic service problems result in lost accounts. We are at that point with two important customers:

- Anderson Techtronics
- BestRight Foundry

We must get their service problems under control immediately or risk loss of either or both accounts. The problem is critical and demands our immediate attention. Refer to previous correspondence and then please map out a planned approach to resolve this problem. Let's meet tomorrow morning first thing. Give me a call this afternoon to confirm this meeting.

Model Memo 8-11

TO: Service Manager

FROM: Sales Manager

SUBJECT: Prompt Service Calls

This memo summarizes the conclusions and plan of action developed by the two of us this morning concerning the subject.

1. To achieve customer satisfaction, service calls must be made within 24 hours of call-in.

2. If it is impossible to complete the call within 24 hours, the client should be called, the problem explained, and alternate arrangements made if possible.

3. The Sales Department will be notified of delays longer than 24 hours.

4. You have agreed to institute a program of logging the time service requests as they are received and when the service call is made.

5. You plan to request the approval of capital funds to purchase two-way radios in all service vehicles to expedite service calls.

6. You are planning certain in-department changes in handling service assignments that should result in improved service-call time response.

Thanks for your understanding and valuable help in this critical matter. Without your assistance a lot of valuable business might be placed in jeopardy.

cc: VP Sales

The close cooperation between Sales and Service Departments is not just a one-way street. The Sales Department has its responsibilities also. Here is a memo that summarizes the steps the Sales Department has agreed to implement.

Model Memo 8-12

TO: Service Manager

FROM: Sales Manager

SUBJECT: Apprising Service Department of Service Problems

I recognize that the Service Department may find it impossible to handle service problems it knows nothing about. Therefore, I am implementing the following procedures immediately:

1. We are providing a simple, easy-to-use form to all sales reps to complete whenever they hear or see a service problem.

2. One copy of the completed form will be forwarded to your department for handling.

3. Our service policy will be carefully explained to all customers. Service charges will be distributed in a letter going out from this department this week.

I expect this to take care of the problems we discussed today. I appreciate your calling them to my attention.

cc: VP Sales

Model Memo 8-13

TO: Service Manager

FROM: Sales Manager

SUBJECT: Service to the Denger Manufacturing Account

Following up our conversation: The breakdown in service to Denger Manufacturing Co. has presented a serious problem to us. Their equipment failure has caused them to miss a deadline and has resulted in considerable overtime charges. Their business means approximately $325M per year. We cannot afford to lose it. I know you are doing everything you can to get this thing under control. This memo has only one purpose: to stress the importance of correcting the problem and to encourage you to get it handled as quickly as possible.

Let me know daily of your progress.

Model Memo 8-14

TO: Service Manager

FROM: Sales Manager

SUBJECT: Arnold Controls Account

The Service Department's performance in correcting the Arnold Controls problem was excellent. Their problem was acute. Our product breakdown meant shutdown of the entire line. Your response time was under one hour. Equipment was repaired in less than three hours. This important customer is happy with our performance.

Thanks! And congratulations!

cc: VP Sales

4. MEMOS TO THE MANUFACTURING DIVISION

As with all interdivision memos, be careful to observe protocol here. If the Manufacturing Division is headed by a VP, and you are the sales manager, it will probably be better to handle manufacturing problems through your V.P. of Marketing. However, in many smaller organizations you may be able to deal directly with the chief of manufacturing without stepping on toes. These memos are then for you.

Model Memo 8-15

TO: Manager of Manufacturing

FROM: Sales Manager

SUBJECT: Opportunity for Improvement, Flat Goods Folder

This date we discussed the need for improvement of the second fold operation of our flat goods unit. The possibility exists to improve the accuracy and consistency of the operation. In addition we might be able to eliminate the time now required of the operator to keep this segment in adjustment.

Competition now has the same problem with this fold as we do. If we can make the changes requested, we will have an important advantage over them with a patented improvement. The improvement is important to our customers and prospects and would command a significant increase in product value.

Time is of the essence in this matter. Competition will surely arrive at the same conclusion in time. Our action now will maintain our marketing edge.

cc: VP, Marketing

Model Memo 8-16

TO: Manager of Manufacturing

FROM: Sales Manager

SUBJECT: Delivery Scheduling

It is imperative that we improve our elapsed time from order placement to shipment. Customer complaints are indicating that it is taking as much as three weeks for orders to be shipped. As you know on five occasions in the past month we have suffered order cancellations because we could not ship when required. You have agreed to take steps to reduce the shipping date to within eight working days of order placement. I recognize it will require at least three weeks to make the necessary changes. In the meantime we will do our best to keep things patched with our customers.

Thanks for your understanding, Tom. This is an extremely critical problem.

cc: VP, Sales

5. MEMOS TO THE CREDIT DEPARTMENT

Ah, the Credit Department! If they would just loosen up on the reins a bit. If they would just not press so hard on my customer who is a bit tardy. As tough as they seem, the credit people do want to work with the Sales Department. And many times they will bend over backward to help if they but know what the situation really is. Frequent memos can be of great assistance to keep the Credit Department informed and to gain its cooperation with Sales.

Memos from Sales to Credit Department typically involve such subjects as securing special terms, explaining extenuating circumstances concerning late payments, or reporting late payments or improvements in payment performance. Included here are the memos you are likely to be called to write.

Memos requesting special terms should quickly convey three items of information: Who the customer is for whom special terms are requested, what terms you feel are in order, and why you feel the terms should be granted. The following memo provides the necessities.

Model Memo 8-17

TO: Credit Manager

FROM: Sales Manager

SUBJECT: Smith Concrete and Contracting

Due to unusual circumstance, I am requesting special terms for our customer, Smith Concrete and Contracting. I recommend that 60-day terms be granted this account. Much of the account's business is with government agencies. These customers normally pay Smith C & C only after a minimum of 60 days. days. These terms will retain a valuable customer and will in the long run, increase our sales to them.

Model Memo 8-18

TO: Credit Manager

FROM: Sales Manager

SUBJECT: Discounted Billing to Steel Fabricating Companies

Sales Department strongly recommends that we bill on a 1%/10, Net/30 with our steel fabricating customers. Most will take as much time paying as they can get. Based on experience with similar industries, a 1% in 10-day discount will materially improve payment performance. If collections are improved by 25 to 30 days, the discount may more than pay for itself in faster cash turnover.

Memos may be used to explain extenuating credit circumstances. For example a memo might be used to pass on to the Credit Department why a customer has become slow to pay. These memos should include information such as who the customer is, what the situation is about which you are writing, why the situation is occurring, and for how long. This memo fills the bill.

Model Memo 8-19

TO: Credit Manager

FROM: Sales Manager

SUBJECT: Laughlin Machine Tool

As you note, Laughlin Machine Tool account has been running about 60 days. This is an unusual situation for them and I have personally investigated the matter.

Here are the reasons:

1. Laughlin has secured a large new customer. This has required a substantial increase in inventory to meet initial needs.

2. Payroll has increased by four persons to meet the needs of the customer.

Laughlin Machine Tool remains a strong customer with a temporary credit problem caused by its rapidly growing business. I would expect the problem to be resolved in 60 days. At that time Laughlin should be seeing payments coming in on the new business they are now writing.

No one likes to report bad news. But at times it becomes necessary in order to protect the company and your reputation. When you learn that a customer has encountered adverse business conditions that will affect his ability to pay, you must, of course, report the findings to the Credit Department for their immediate action. Speed is often of the essence here. A telephone call first may be in order, followed by a memo which formalizes your conversation and gives some written record of your action.

Model Memo 8-20

TO: Credit Manager

FROM: Sales Manager

SUBJECT: Johnson's Quick Print

The above account is encountering financial reverses which place our company at risk. This has been caused by a poor accounts receivable policy and several rather large losses. Recommend that Johnson be placed on a C.O.D. basis until the situation improves.

cc: Sales Representative

And when the situation improves, you owe it to your customer to report that situation also.

Model Memo 8-21

TO: Credit Manager

FROM: Sales Manager

SUBJECT: Johnson's Quick Print

I have had a conversation with the accountant for Johnson Quick Print. He informs me that the accounts receivable there is gradually being improved. Total receivables are only one-third what they were when the pay problem occurred. Average pay period is now 20 days. Based on this, I recommend that Johnson be considered for credit terms under a restricted basis.

9

LETTERS THAT LOCK IN THE SALE

9

LETTERS THAT LOCK
IN THE SALE

Perhaps nothing is more frustrating to salespeople than to have a sale fall apart after it is successfully completed. The sales rep walks away from the customer's office with order in hand. But the next day the customer calls and says something like, "I've been thinking it over. Why don't you hold up on that order for a while." Of course you can require earnest money up front to head off that problem, but wouldn't the effect be much better if the customer never entertained such thoughts of cancellation at all? The problem is called buyer's remorse and every salesperson has encountered it.

A timely letter from the sales rep or the sales manager will often head off buyer's remorse. Such a letter seeks to reinforce the customer's decision to buy your product and assist him in deriving the greatest possible satisfaction from its use.

1. CONGRATULATIONS ON YOUR PURCHASE

Something of one's ego is tied up with every buying decision. We like to feel we have made a good decision. With it goes the feeling that we are intelligent, astute, drive a hard bargain. Reinforcing these feelings in the purchaser assists in reducing the tendency for buyer's remorse. As a sales manager you should train your salespeople to write such letters as these after the sale is complete. Or the same type of letter can be sent from the sales manager's office.

Model Letter 9-1

Dear _____ :

Thank you for your recent order. It is always a pleasure to do business again with a valued customer.

I hope it means that our team of salespeople, office staff, and service and rental personnel understand you and your organization and are delivering our "product" to you in a way and at a price that is comfortable for you.

Please continue to take advantage of the many ways   **(a)**
in which we can assist you . . . and feel free to call me whenever I personally may be of help to you.

Our goal is to merit the right to do continual and increasing business with you.

Thank you again for your recent order.

Sincerely,

Alternate Wording:

(a) We aim to deliver not just a product but also the benefits it will produce for you. Our service and technical staff are available to provide advice and assistance to be sure you get the full benefit of the product.

If your product or service is of the type that is purchased for future use rather than an immediate necessity, you are probably particularly concerned about heading off "buyer's remorse" and reassuring the purchaser of the wisdom of his purchase.

The sales manager who wrote this letter knows the value of following up after the sale and reassuring the buyer.

Model Letter 9-2

Dear Mr. & Mrs. _____:

Your foresight and consideration for your family are clearly proven by the enclosed agreement covering a Family Memorial Estate in _____ Memorial Park.

Your Memorial Counselor joins me in assuring you that in years to come your family will appreciate the wisdom of this move and recognize that you made a sound investment in many respects. I know it will give you deep personal satisfaction and peace of mind to have taken this step, and I earnestly hope no occasion will arise for actual use of your family estate for many, many years.

Sincerely,

Model Letter 9-3

Dear _____:

Your decision to stock the _____ line of hair dryers puts you on the sales team with over 1,600 other retailers across America.

Bill Martin, your Sales Representative, and I join forces to assure you that your decision has been a wise one. The experience of those 1,600 retailers tells us you can expect rapid customer acceptance of the _____ line due to our extensive advertising program. The engineered quality and quality control steps ensure complete customer satisfaction and a minimum of adjustment and service problems. Finally, our pricing policy will provide you with a significant profit contribution to your business.

Welcome to the _____ team!

Sincerely,

In some lines of business, after-the-sale support is particularly important. The writer of this letter believes the retailer needs to be reminded of the backup he receives from the manufacturer along with the quality products he buys for resale.

Model Letter 9-4

Dear _____:

Thank you for the courtesy you showed our representative, _____, the other day and for your order.

Enclosed are advertising slicks to help you in the development of promotions. I know _____ left a kit of promotional ideas and materials for you. She told me you had several ideas for advertising and promotions and thought these slicks would also be of help.

Don't hesitate to get in touch with _____ or me if you have any questions or need additional assistance. Our job is to make selling our product a profitable pleasure for you.

Sincerely,

Model Letter 9-5

Dear _____:

Thank you for the opportunity of getting together on Monday.

I was sorry to hear you are having difficulty moving our model _____ and am canceling the balance of your order for that model as you requested. As we agreed we will work with you to merchandise your present inventory of 200 cases. Al will be calling on you next week to suggest a promotion used by several other dealers which resulted in a high level of sales. Al will also discuss an order for the other _____ products which you mentioned would retail well in your area.   (a)

Your willingness to work with us is most appreciated, and we will put forth our best effort to earn this confidence.

Sincerely,

Alternate Wording:

(a) If, after 30 days of using this promotional plan, you still have inventory, we will accept it with no freight-back cost to you. In that event, Al will get proof-of-delivery from you so we can issue credit and invoice the new customer.

2. SELLING ADDITIONAL SERVICES AND PRODUCTS

Sometimes we are so busy selling new customers that we forget the rich opportunity that is often present with our present ones. Many times additional sales to present customers are the simplest to make since the customer knows your company and is a satisfied user of your products. Perhaps you can get all of his business rather than 35%. Maybe there are products in your line that will also fit his needs of which he knows little.

The letters below include both a sales approach involving a specific product and the more general "shotgun" approach to sell the entire line.

Model Letter 9-6

Dear _____:

At the suggestion of our representative, _____, I am pleased to provide the specifications for our Grade 8 Alloy Cap Screws. I have included the spec sheet for this product. You will note that the product meets all SAE and ASTM standards as well as military standards.

The excellent quality of our product line is only part of the story as we hope your experience with us has confirmed.

98% of our orders are shipped the same day they are received. Our service people know the importance of satisfying you, our customer, and they work hard at getting your order filled on time and accurately.

_____, your sales rep, is charged with the responsibility for understanding your company's fastener needs. He now has more than five years of experience with you in building that understanding.

The result is that we are in a position to provide you with the quality of product, service, and technical assistance you need and expect from a fastener supplier. We appreciate your business and hope you will rely on us to an increasing degree in the future.

Should you require additional information, we are ready to assist you. Thank you for your inquiry. **(a)**

Sincerely,

Alternate Wording:

(a) Our representative will be calling on you shortly to provide any additional information you require and to determine if this product fits your particular situation.

Model Letter 9-7

Dear _____ :

Congratulations on your purchase of _____ You are now the owner of the finest appliance made and can look forward to years of enjoyment.

This quality machine will serve you for years to come. It has been designed to require minimum maintenance. We suggest a yearly "checkup" to allow a qualified technician to make minor adjustments and insure that this fine appliance remains in like-new condition. A brochure describing our service program is attached along with a service agreement. We hope that you will sign the agreement and return it to us and allow us to keep your fine appliance performing at peak efficiency for years at a very modest cost.

Sincerely,

Model Letter 9-8

Dear _____ :

We value your business and would like to extend credit privileges to your company. The benefits of being the holder of a _____ Credit Card are:

- You can receive a discount on your regular rates.
- The need to carry cash for rental deposits is eliminated.

- As a member of the _____ family of credit-card holders, you will receive V.I.P. service.
- Ease cash flow problems that tie up valuable funds.

To become a _____ National Account, complete the application and return it to me in the enclosed envelope today. Thank you.

Sincerely,

Model Letter 9-9

Dear _____:

Looking for that added profit opportunity? Here's an important one that will fit in with the _____ line you are now marketing. This new product has all the features required to be a successful direct mail product. The price is right, it is a quality product, it is aimed at the expanding do-it-yourself market, it is UL approved, it has a better price point. A catalog page is enclosed. **(a)**

Our representative, _____, will be calling on you next week to explore the potential of this product in your market.

Sincerely,

Alternate Wording:

(a) This new product has all the features you look for in a self-service store product.

Model Letter 9-10

Dear _____:

It's been a good year for you and your company. Increased sales and profits were rare in a tight economy and competitive market.

Although many elements were undoubtedly involved in your company's performance, I'm sure we are agreed that your imaginative use of our service was one contributing factor.

Perhaps you can contribute even further to your company's success by utilizing another of our services. We can now provide a low-cost, low-paper-work system that will help you to effectively manage all of your receivables, reduce your receivable and bad debt level, and improve your cash flow.

Dave will contact you next week to explore how this system might fit into your operation.

Again, my sincere compliments on your personal accomplishments and your company's outstanding performance during the past year.

Sincerely,

10

LETTERS THAT OVERCOME THE CUSTOMER'S RESISTANCE TO CHANGE

10

LETTERS THAT OVERCOME THE CUSTOMER'S RESISTANCE TO CHANGE

The more things change the more they stay the same. But the change we manage always seems to be the kind that upsets our sales force, our distributors, dealers, service dealers, and customers. Price change — think it's going down? Of course not — another increase. One of your salespeople transferred/promoted? A low producer, unpopular with customers, a lot of trouble, right? Wrong — your highest producer, a customer favorite, your favorite. That's the way it goes. Nobody said it was easy.

Change is necessary even when customers resist. Products change, prices must change, people change, marketing policies change. Since you can't eliminate change, you must prepare customers to make the transition as painlessly as possible.

Any change is an opportunity to contact past and present prospects, present customers, or existing accounts. The communication should stress a new opportunity provided by change in your company or product. Involving the sales force and getting their input for both the points which should be stressed in the letter and who it should be sent to will strengthen this approach. Also, the salesperson should receive a copy of the letter before it is sent to the distributor, dealer, prospect, or customer. These letters can be important sales tools leading to sales when changes occur.

1. ANNOUNCING THE PRICE INCREASE

It sometimes seems like the most common change in the world is the price increase. Probably every sales manager has written at least one letter announcing a price increase. Some of you may have had a lot of practice on this one. But it doesn't get any easier with practice.

We don't want this letter to come across as cold and impersonal, with a take-it-or-leave-it attitude.

Most really effective price increase letters have three common elements:

1. They stress the company's efforts to hold the line on prices;
2. The review the pressures causing the increase;
3. They stress areas where the company has been successful holding down prices.

Model Letter 10-1

Dear _____:

It's no secret that costs in our industry have been climbing. We've been able to hold the line on our prices during the last couple of years with only one price adjustment on our _____ line. Over the past five years we have succeeded in avoiding mid-season price adjustments. It hasn't been easy. We've cut costs through innovation and more efficient processes. We've replaced old, labor-intensive methods with investment in the most modern equipment. We've sacrificed our own profit, cutting margins close to breakeven — and below on some models.

This year we have been forced to make a limited **(a)**
number of price adjustments. The only alternative
would be reduced quality. We will continue to provide
the quality standard of the industry. We will continue
to provide top quality parts and service in all lines. We
have been able to hold the price line on 80% of our
line through innovations and cost reductions. The
attached price list reflects the lines where changes
are necessary. We will continue to honor all orders
received before May 15th at old prices. Please contact
your representative or me if you have any questions
or if we can be of assistance in any way.

Sincerely,

Alternate Wording:

(a) We will continue to hold the price line on 80% of our products
this year through innovations and cost reductions. On the few
products where small increases were necessary, we continue
to provide top quality at a competitive price.

Model Letter 10-2

Dear _____:

We know how aware you are of the increasing raw
material costs in our industry. You may have
wondered how we've managed to hold the line with
no price increases for the last nine months. We've
done it with manufacturing innovations and cost
reductions in our own processes.

We have reached the point, however, where even
with the improvements we continue to make, the
increasing cost of necessary purchased materials
forces us to adjust prices.

We promise to maintain the superior quality you
expect from us and continue to innovate in order to
reduce our own costs wherever possible, thereby
keeping our prices to our customers as low as
possible.

We are proud of our reputation for the best quality per dollar in the industry and we will continue to earn that distinction.

The attached price list becomes effective September 1. We will continue to honor all orders received before that date at the old prices.

Please contact our sales representatives or call me if you have any questions or need assistance.

Sincerely,

We never send notices such as these to customers without prior notification of the sales force. Since the sales force must be completely supportive of a price change or the company will lose customers, plenty of two-way communication is called for. Here is a letter sent to the sales force with the price increase announcement letter several days before the announcement is sent to customers.

Model Letter 10-3

Dear _____:

As you know, we have known for months that a price increase was inevitable. We knew the amounts of increases a couple of weeks ago. At our meeting last week, we agreed the increases were reasonable and saleable. We went over the planned steps of announcing the price adjustment to customers. The first step in the announcement to customers is a letter which will be sent to them this Friday for delivery early next week. A copy of that letter is enclosed. Please review the letter as part of your preparation for your calls next week. Use the specially designed one-use call cards to send back customer reactions.

The letter is pretty conventional and says about what we expected. Give me a call if you want to discuss the letter before making follow-up calls. Otherwise I look forward to feedback on the reaction of your customers next week.

Sincerely,

2. SELLING CHANGES IN THE DISCOUNT STRUCTURE

Quantity or price discounts for distributor, dealer, or final user/customers is a very similar subject to price. This directly affects the profit/income and easily becomes an emotional issue. Unless the change in discount policy is obviously in their favor, customers will resist changes in discounts. We must get them to see an advantage for themselves to insure acceptance of a new discount structure.

Model Letter 10-4

Dear _____:

It's always enjoyable to talk to a loyal customer of many years. Thank you for the time you spent with me on the phone yesterday. Your insight into the importance of our fair treatment of customers in the growth of the company in recent years made a great impression on me.

We are doing our best to insure continued fair treatment of our customers. Recently, we faced a real problem due to our long-standing policy of a 2% cash discount for payment in 10 days. Many customers **(a)** were taking the discount and paying in 30, 45, or 60 days. Our 2%/10 net 30 credit policy was not only destroying our profit margin and forcing us to consider across-the-board price increases affecting all of our customers, but it was also causing slow deliveries. Our Credit Department was attempting to fairly enforce our terms and were holding up **(b)** shipments until they were sure of the status of some shipments. This led to some obvious problems for some of our best customers, including your company.

Our solution has been to reduce prices by 2%, eliminate the cash discount, and enforce the penalty on late payment. The effect of this policy is to give the cash discount to our early pay accounts and deny it to others. In general our best customers have expressed satisfaction with this policy and it has eliminated all late delivery problems.

Thank you for your interest in this policy. We do review our credit terms and policy periodically and we will certainly take your preferences into account in the future.

Sincerely,

Alternate Wording:

(a) We had provided cash discounts the past couple of years, but recently were forced to discontinue that practice when many customers began taking unearned discounts.

(b) Some needed shipments were held up until invoices were settled and, in general, an unpleasant condition existed.

Model Letter 10-5

Dear _____:

I enjoyed talking with you the other day. I appreciated your ideas and I expect to use the one promotion you had such success with last year this spring on a national basis. This will give you a chance to use it again with, as you said, a bit of "company money in the pot funding a promotion that makes money for both the distributor and the manufacturer."

Thank you also for your comment that we have always been "straight shooters" in dealings with distributors. We respect our distributors as solid business people and superior sales organizations.

I'm sorry we offended you last month when we denied the full "three-step" discount on a small shipment. The question was whether you had a dealer and a service organization or service dealer in that territory. We recognize that you have always been straight with us. We never meant to infer that **(a)** you were trying to get something extra you hadn't earned. I apologize for the misunderstanding. But, as I explained on the phone, I can't promise it won't happen again as we begin strictly enforcing our distributor discount policy.

We intend to allow full distributor discount in territories where distributors have established dealers and service outlets and deny them in territories where the distributor is functioning only as a dealer. This is in the long-range best interest of the **(b)** distributors. As you are well aware, some manufacturers have indiscriminately allowed full discounts resulting in dealers poaching sales in distributors' territory, using their extra discount to cut price and destroy margins. We do not intend to allow this to happen. Your Regional Representative will provide further details on our current campaign to enforce our distributor policy when she calls on you next week.

Thanks again for your understanding. I'm sure you will agree with what we are doing when you discuss the policy fully with Ms. Turner. Please also provide her full details of your spring promotion so we can begin implementing it on a national basis this spring.

Sincerely,

Alternate Wording:

(a) You are aware of the strategy some manufacturers have used in attempting to get as many outlets as possible without regard for quality of distribution. They have allowed full discount to all, making it impossible for distributors to sign up dealers and ultimately making it impossible for distributors to make a profit due to unfair price competition from backyard operators.

(b) An undesirable side effect of our compaign to strictly enforce legitimate distributor discounts will be the occasional denial of full discount on one of your shipments.

3. PRODUCT DISCONTINUANCE

Discontinuing a line can generate protest from salespeople, distributors/dealers, and retail customers. No matter how obviously a product has become a loser in the view of the home office, a few dedicated customers will continue to see it as the greatest invention ever offered the civilized world. Ideally, you would like to switch them over to another product that is comparable. But since customers may be reluctant to change, it may take a careful application of human relations to keep them buying.

Dear _____:

Thank you for using our Model XX over the past ten years. Although literally thousands of our customers also loyally purchased that model for years, the last couple of years' demand has dropped dramatically as customers switched to the Model XXX.

We have continued to produce and inventory Model XX for those who preferred it to the improved Model XXX. However, we have reached the point where it is **(a)** just not possible to stock Model XX at such a low demand level. We are sure you will find the Model XXX more than worth the modest additional cost. Others found it more cost effective and literally demanded its improved features.

Ms. Jan Rhode will call this week for an appointment to demonstrate the improved model. Thank you again for your business. We look forward to providing quality products to meet your needs for years to come.

Sincerely,

Alternate Wording:

(a) We don't believe in change for the sake of change. We believe you will be most pleased with the cost effective improvements in the Model XXX.

4. INTRODUCING A NEW SALESPERSON

If it is true that nothing in life is certain except change, we can be absolutely certain there will be turnover in the sales force. Customers may have become comfortable with the salesperson or they just dislike any disruption. We need to assure them they will be as well or better served by our company in the future. When a salesperson leaves to join a competitor and we expect him to attempt to take our customers with him, this is crucial.

```
┌─────────────────────┐
│                     │
│                     │
│   PROVIDE PHOTO OF   │
│   SALESPERSON HERE   │
│                     │
│                     │
│                     │
└─────────────────────┘
```

Dear _____:

We are pleased to announce the appointment of Paul Sield as your Account Executive.

During his seven years with our organization Paul **(a)** has worked in our Service, Rental, and Sales Departments and has a wealth of technical knowledge and practical experience implementing innovative production solutions on major projects for our customers. You will find Paul not only highly qualified to serve your needs, but also friendly and enthusiastic, and eager to work with you to find ways to increase the efficiency and profitability of your manufacturing processes. Paul is an individual about whom we can say quite literally the expertise of your Account Executive is an important part of the package of value we deliver to you.

Paul will contact you within a week to arrange an appointment to become familiar with your company and manufacturing processes. If you have immediate needs please phone him at XXX-XXXX.

Paul and I and our entire company promise to remain attentive to your every need.

Sincerely,

Alternate Wording:

(a) Paul comes to us with seven years' experience in our industry. He has practical knowledge on the service side of our business and has proven technical competence with all of the equipment you are using.

Model Letter 10-8

Dear _____ :

Sharon B. has been promoted to District Manager of our Los Angeles office. We know you enjoyed doing business with Sharon for the past three years. We're sure you can understand why the company decided she will be of even more value to our customers with expanded responsibilities.

But I know you hate to see her go as much as I do because a knowledgeable and competent salesperson of that caliber is hard to find. However, her replacement is an experienced customer service relations representative from our Des Moines office, John D. I have followed this man's career for a couple of years and requested him as soon as Sharon's promotion was certain. Believe me, John's clients in Des Moines hated to lose him.

John has been working with Sharon for a week now, and they'll have two more weeks to make sure John knows all of the customers and their needs before Sharon leaves.

John is a professional with a strong background in our business and both Sharon and I know you'll enjoy doing business with him.

Sincerely,

Model Letter 10-9

Dear _____ :

You're invited to a party! We're having a get-together and dinner next Thursday to congratulate Chuck Wesson and give him a proper send-off to Denver where he will be Regional Sales Manager.   **(a)**

I know you like Chuck's style and appreciate his technical expertise. We are both lucky that we are getting an experienced replacement from Omaha. His name is Dan Briggs. He has been working with **(b)** Chuck for a week, getting familiar with the area. He has impressed both Chuck and me with his competence, knowledge, and energy in the short time we've worked with him. His manager hates to lose him and I'm told he has a "fan club" among his customers similar to Chuck. So join me and a few of Chuck's other customers next Thursday to meet Dan Briggs and to wish Chuck well in his new assignment.

Sincerely,

Alternate Wording:

(a) Chuck Wesson has been promoted to Regional Manager of our Denver office! I know we agree that no salesman in our company could deserve the promotion more than Chuck, but you probably hate to see him go as much as I do.

(b) We are both in luck, however, because Dan Briggs who is transferring here from Omaha has a reputation for competence and service to his customers similar to Chuck's.

5. INTRODUCING A NEW SERVICE REPRESENTATIVE

Sometimes customers become as attached to a very capable and personable serviceperson as they are to their sales rep, perhaps moreso. If that serviceperson is transferred or leaves the organization, we need to put a lot of care and thought into breaking the news to the customers and introducing a replacement.

Model Letter 10-10

Dear _____:

You will receive a complimentary service call next **(a)** week and you'll meet your new Service Representative, Ken Terry. He will phone this week to arrange a convenient time.

Ken comes with an excellent background. He has a base of experience as our in-house service specialist for the past two years. While there he worked directly under our Service Manager for this Division. In addition he has completed every course provided by the company for maintaining your equipment. In short, he knows your equipment and how to keep it running at peak efficiency.

I know you thought highly of John Alton, who has **(a)** left the company. I believe you will find Ken every bit as accommodating and easy to work with, as well as being technically skilled. He and I both want to do everything necessary to provide you with complete satisfaction with our equipment.

Sincerely,

Alternate Wording:

(a) You will be pleased to hear that John Alton, your Service Representative has been promoted to the position of Service Manager for the Eastern Division. His promotion was largely due to the outstanding service he has been providing your company and others these past three years.

6. DISCONTINUING ADVERTISING OR PROMOTION SUPPORT

Whether you have a direct sales force, distributor/dealer, exclusive dealer, or rep/agent organization, they quickly become attached to company-provided or subsidized advertising and sales promotion support. That makes such support much more difficult to discontinue than to initiate. But circumstances do arise that make continuation of some programs costly and ill-advised. This letter lets the affected sales force down gently.

Model Letter 10-11

Dear _____:

For the past 12 months we have been supporting our dealers in the Bismark area with regular newspaper ads promoting our _____ line. This trial effort was intended to determine if the area would respond to intensive product advertising of this type. The indication provided by you and other area dealers is that this advertising effort has not yielded sufficient results to warrant continuing.

The April ad will be our last of the current type. In its place we plan to increase our point-of-sale promotions. Your representative will outline the new promotion program during his next call.

Tests with other dealers indicate good customer response to the new program. Sales increases of 10% to 18% have been reported. I think you will want to participate.

Sincerely,

7. ANNOUNCING "SPECIALS"

You know it is not safe to assume the sales force will see how much help a promotional program will be to them. You have to promote the promotion to the salespeople. Any price reduction, sale, or offer of extras deserves a general promotion effort to the direct sales force, dealer organization, and customers.

Model Letter 10-12

Dear _____:

Remember the fast start we got off to the first quarter this past year? Remember the "FAST START 19__" promotion program? We think there may have been a connection between the 18% increase in sales last year over the same time period a year earlier. So we're repeating the same program this year.

A complete description of the program is attached. We believe we learned last year that your dealers will participate in the extra advertising and pace their purchases to the increase they experience at retail in January and February. In March last year they began stocking up, ordering at almost double their normal rate. Some dealers continued the program on their own through April. Others just went back to normal prices and terms and kept the differential in margin. You know which of your dealers followed which course of action. I've attached last year's dealer orders of January through May for last year, and you can guess which ones extended the promotion a month. The difference in April and May orders to restock show the effect of extending through April. So plan in advance how you might sell all your dealers on continuing the program an extra month on their own.

We'll discuss how to make the most of the FAST START program this year at our District sales meeting next Monday. Review your experiences from last year and bring your suggestions.

Sincerely,

Promotions also provide an opportunity to get your salespeople to revive warm prospects, and go after new ones. This auto dealership revived some of last month's prospects with this letter.

Model Letter 10-13

Dear _____:

I was pleased to learn that you recently visited our dealership to discuss a possible new automobile purchase.

But I was naturally disappointed that we apparently   **(a)** could not satisfy your requirements.

Each Autumn we celebrate the season with our "Octoberfest Days." We have a large selection of the most popular models available at reduced prices for this annual event. I have reviewed your needs with your salesman Jerry _____, and I'm sure he can meet your requirements during this sale. Please come to our Octoberfest and present this letter to Jerry. He will do his best to match your needs.

Sincerely,

Alternate Wording:

(a) Although I was disappointed to hear we could not satisfy your requirements at the time of your visit, I'm delighted to invite you to a special event which should enable you to find **exactly** what you want.

8. INTRODUCING A NEW PRODUCT

When a new product is introduced, the new features and benefits must be sold, especially if the emphasis is somewhat different than past products offered. The first letter was written to automobile dealers emphasizing the advantages of more extensive available options in the new model. The second letter points out unique capabilities of a new product to users.

Model Letter 10-14

Dear _____:

The success of the new _____ re-emphasizes a marketing fact. The fact is that most customers want personalized comfort and appearance items on any car they buy. The average customer is willing to pay the small additional cost for these items if he or she feels that they will add to the overall pleasure of owning and driving the car. We sometimes become so price-conscious ourselves that we forget this fact.

This year's _____ is a totally refined product by any standard. It has economy, reliability, time-tested value. Take a close look at the optional accessory packages. Personalized luxury may be emphasized in the way one floor model or demo is equipped. Display another equipped for the enthusiast. Sportier accessory packages add that touch of pizzaz!

We've got the product! Let's display it so buyers can see that they can make their new _____ as distinctively their own individual creation as they wish.

Sincerely,

Model Letter 10-15

Dear _____:

How many times have you received complaints that were the result of the dispenser and not your material?

We have developed a line of sprayers that can handle even problem materials like fish oils and wettable powders.

Don't take my word for it. Our representative will call next week to demonstrate the capabilities of this new product. We know that you will have to see it to believe it!

Sincerely,

11

TELLING YOUR CUSTOMERS YOU APPRECIATE THEIR BUSINESS

11

TELLING YOUR CUSTOMERS YOU APPRECIATE THEIR BUSINESS

The competitive nature of business frequently makes it difficult to differentiate a business from others offering substantially the same product or service. In such instances it is often the small differences that make a big impact on the customer. A small plus in service offered or a unique twist to a product feature can give a company a competitive edge. An important competitive edge is available to the sales organization that takes the time and effort to show appreciation for the customer's business. The real estate agent is likely to be remembered long after the sale when she sends a note of thanks and a welcome mat to a family after they move into their new home. And who do you think the family will remember when they get transfered out a few years later and must sell that home? The auto salesperson will be likely to increase repeat business when making it a practice to call a customer 60 or 90 days after a sale to see how the customer likes his new purchase.

Most buyers have a variety of places they could go in making a purchase and they know it. When they give you their business they are doing you a favor. When you show them you realize and appreciate the favor they have given, you will be cementing a relationship that is likely to endure.

Appreciation letters are appropriate from either sales representative or sales manager. If you send such letters, it is a good idea to apprise the sales rep of what you are doing.

1. APPRECIATION FOR YEARS OF BUSINESS

One appropriate time to say "thanks" is on a business anniversary. Some sales managers keep a file and write appreciation letters on first, fifth, tenth, or whatever anniversary of the first transaction between their company and the customer.

Model Letter 11-1

Dear _____:

The other day I glanced at the first correspondence between our two companies and realized that it was five years ago that we first had the opportunity to serve you.

It made me think. I couldn't remember when I had dropped you a note just to let you know we appreciate your business.

We do appreciate your business and look forward to serving you for the next five years.

Sincerely,

Model Letter 11-2

Dear _____:

This is an anniversary of sorts and an important one for me! One year ago this month our two companies did business together for the first time.

We have enjoyed the relationship and want to thank you for the business you have placed with us. We want you to know we will continue to do our best to provide the service which justifies your faith in us. We believe we gained understanding of your particular needs during the past year which will enable us to be even more useful to you as a supplier in the next 12 months.

Sincerely,

Any holiday also provides an opportunity to say "thanks" for being a customer. The sales manager who provided this letter feels that a personal letter at Christmas has more sales impact with customers than a conventional card. The letter is typed on stationery with "old-fashioned Christmas scene" art instead of the company letterhead, and it is hand-signed over the company name and sales manager's name and title.

Model Letter 11-3

Dear _____:

If we ran a general store in a small town and you were a near neighbor and customer, here's what could happen.

As the Christmas season approached we would find more frequent opportunities to chat with you. We would ask if all the children would be home for Christmas and whether you were spending the day at Aunt Kate's or if it was at your place this year.

We would make a point of thanking you for your business during the year. "It's been a good year for us" we'd say, "but only because of loyal friends like you — and we sure do appreciate the business you give us year in and year out." We'd shake hands and a stronger bond of friendship would be cemented.

We hope we have recaptured a little of that simple, warm, direct relationship in our dealings with you. We thank you — we enjoy working with you — and we appreciate your cordial attitude toward us. We hope you enjoy a most pleasant Holiday Season!

Sincerely,

2. APPRECIATION FOR A LARGE ORDER

When a buyer places an order which is unusually large or which is unusually important for the buyer or company, a letter from the sales manager can be reassuring.

Model Letter 11-4

Dear _____:

Thank you for the order you placed with our representative, John _____, last Thursday. We appreciate the confidence you have shown in our organization through this order.

Your order is being filled right now and I am working with our shipping personnel to be sure everything is shipped exactly as you specified.

John _____ will call on you next Thursday to make sure everything in the shipment meets with your approval. We believe you have made a wise purchase.

Sincerely,

Model Letter 11-5

Dear _____:

Thanks for taking the time to meet with our representative, Leslie _____, on a Saturday morning. She communicated to me how important the immediate use of this program is to you and your company.

We are now in the process of setting it up and making it happen. Leslie will be back to you with the initial plans on Wednesday, and the program will be complete by (date) as you specified.

Again thanks, and it's great to be doing business with you.

Sincerely,

3. APPRECIATION FOR COOPERATION IN TIME OF SHORTAGE OR OTHER UNUSUAL SITUATION

Things don't always work smoothly after the sale. Raw material shortages, strikes, or unforseen problems in production can complicate the buyer-seller relationship. When these problems occur the sales rep works hard to keep the sale glued together. When the rep succeeds, it is usually because the buyer is convinced that your product is worth waiting for or that your company will come through in the end. Once convinced, the buyer often cooperates with the sales organization rather than canceling the order.

This kind of cooperation deserves a special thanks from the sales manager. These are tough letters to write but worth it. There is a temptation to "let well enough alone" when your company has performed its part of the agreement, hoping the buyer will forget the difficulties involved in the sale. This sales manager chose to emphasize the positive and use the difficulties involved in the sale to cement the relationship.

Model Letter 11-6

Dear _____:

I thought I heard a loud sigh of relief from your office last Friday when our shipment arrived. Even though we are over 50 miles apart, I'm sure you heard my own sigh of relief all the way to your office. And Jim is a new man. He was beginning to look ten years older worrying about your order — and so was I.

None of us could have anticipated the material shortage when you placed the order but that didn't make the last few weeks any more comfortable for any of us. I want to tell you how much Jim and I appreciated your cooperation in this matter. We appreciate your believing the quality of our product was worth waiting for and we intend to justify your faith in us and our product in the future.

Our company has learned from experience and has taken steps which insure that this situation will not recur. I'd like to tell you about the changes we've made.

I feel that we have been "through the fire" together and would like to meet you and Jim for dinner next Tuesday to celebrate our common victory over the material shortage. Jim will pick you up at your office if that is convenient.

I'll call you Monday to confirm the time.

Sincerely,

4. APPRECIATION FOR FIRST ORDER

A conventional but important time to let customers know you appreciate their business is immediately after they place their first order. If you let them know they are important to you at the onset, repeat orders may come sooner and easier.

Model Letter 11-7

Dear _____:

Both Mr. _____, our sales representative, and I would like to express our sincere appreciation for the courtesies extended to us at the time of our recent visit.

We look forward to the pleasure of serving you.

If there is any way we can be of assistance, please feel free to call on us at any time. **(a)**

Sincerely,

Alternate Wording:

(a) We truly appreciate the business with which you have favored us, and look forward to the pleasure of serving you for a long time to come.

Model Letter 11-8

Dear _____:

We would like to express our appreciation for the kindness extended to Ms. _____ on the occasion of her recent visit.

Ms. _____ indicated that you are interested in **(a)** knowing more about our returns policy and about our products liability coverage.

First of all, we protect our customer's inventories by seeing to it that any merchandise which is surplus to your requirements or becomes obsolete for your equipment may be returned for full credit, providing, of course, it is in new and saleable condition.

Our Products Liability Insurance coverage is indicated by the attached Certificate of Insurance which, I am sure, is self-explanatory.

We trust that this is the information you require, and, in the meantime, we would like to express our appreciation for your business. We look forward to the pleasure of serving you in the future.

Sincerely,

Alternate Wording:

(a) Ms. _____ indicated that you are interested in the technical specifications of our zinc irridite plating process. I've attached information which points out the product quality and economic advantages of this process.

5. APPRECIATION FOR A TESTIMONIAL

Heartfelt testimonials are worth money. Yet a satisfied customer is likely to give them free of charge. For such a valuable gift the customer deserves an expression of gratitude.

Model Letter 11-9

Dear _____:

Thank you for your kind remarks about our company in your presentation to the bankers association last Thursday.

The experiences you related obviously came straight **(a)** from your heart and I believe had a real effect on your audience. I know you are as happy to be associated with this company as a customer as I am as an employee. I had the feeling you were speaking for thousands of satisfied customers and this came through to the bankers, I'm sure.

I'm proud to represent a company that produces the results you described so well and I'm proud to be associated with customers like you who support a product and company they believe in.

Thanks again.

Sincerely,

Alternate Wording:

(a) You worked hard at remaining neutral in your comments and rightly so. At the same time your strong feelings for our company and the services we have provided your bank came through loud and clear. Your unbiased comments had a stronger impact on the audience because of your approach. After the meeting I had several requests for additional information on the program. Five bank officers invited our people to come by to make a complete presentation. I'll keep you posted on the results.

Model Letter 11-10

Dear _____:

I want to thank you and everyone in your organization for choosing Dave _____ as the outstanding salesperson serving _____ Hospital for 19__.

I respect Dave's professional approach to selling and am proud he is part of our organization. I particularly appreciated one paragraph in the letter you sent Dave informing him of the award:

> "As you know, Dave, product-oriented salespeople are easy to find, but customer-oriented ones are not. Today's hospitals need more than just commodities; we need information too. As a customer-oriented salesperson, you are aware of the total needs."

Our entire organization is proud that you have chosen Dave as the outstanding salesperson serving you. All of us intend to continue to do our best to provide the quality products and services you have come to expect from Dave and our company.

Sincerely,

12

MODEL LETTERS THAT TURN CUSTOMER COMPLAINTS INTO NEW BUSINESS

12

MODEL LETTERS THAT TURN CUSTOMER COMPLAINTS INTO NEW BUSINESS

Once upon a time most major retailers and downtown department stores had a desk or service window with a large sign above it that said clearly, "COMPLAINTS." The complaint desk is rarely seen in today's fast-moving shopping mall environment. Perhaps that is because today's consumer doesn't require the ritual of smiling, sympathetic understanding and reassurance once dispensed by the "complaint" desk. Or everyone is so rushed that they prefer the speed of telephone exchange of information or exchanging computer code numbers with the assurance that a credit will appear on the next bill.

Not many years ago, a two-hour lunch was often the conventional environment for a salesperson to listen and empathize while an industrial buyer described the hardship a product imperfection caused the company.

A skillful sales rep could usually reassure the buyer that the supplier company would not allow the problem to occur again. But business mores and customs have changed and buyers often don't allow salespeople the face-to-face time they once did. Especially not when the salesperson has caused them a problem. Written communication has become more important in handling complaints.

Face-to-face communication remains the preferred environment for dealing with complaints. And the telephone provides two-way communication and timeliness and remains a first-line tool for handling complaints. The letter is also an important communication tool because it permits an official confirmation of the company's understanding of the problem and what will be done to correct the situation.

Proper handling of complaints requires three major steps:

1. Acknowledge the customer's point of view. Customers don't necessarily expect sympathy, but they do expect us to understand how they feel. First step, tell the customer you understand. This will take much of the emotion out of the complaint. The customer feels the seller is willing to work out a solution.

2. Determine or review the facts. If you don't have all the facts pertaining to the complaint, use the telephone to get them. If this is impractical, use a letter of inquiry. A sample letter is provided on page 196. If you are providing or confirming a solution to the customer's problem, review the facts briefly. This step assures the customer that you understand the situation and also provides him or her an opportunity to correct, if necessary, where you may have your facts wrong.

3. Indicate how you will resolve the complaint. The customer usually just wants action and doesn't care who is to blame. Indicate what is to be done and when.

The letters in this section follow this format in handling complaints.

1. RESPONDING TO A PRODUCT COMPLAINT

This letter was written to a dealer complaining the product wasn't selling.

Model Letter 12-1

Dear _____:

I can understand your concern with slow-moving inventory as you explained in our phone conversation today. I've discussed the situation with your area representative, Jack Mobley, as I promised. Jack will phone you the next day or so and arrange to meet at your earliest convenience.

I'll leave it to Jack to go over the details with you but **(a)** he and I believe we can resolve this situation to your satisfaction. We are as concerned as you that you have sold only three cases since you took on our line six months ago. Normally, we would have received two reorders of at least the same amount as the original order by now. Our company is losing volume just as you are.

Jack will go over your requirements and the buying preferences of your particular neighborhood. You know your own trade. We believe Jack may have been too quick with a recommendation of product that has been "hot" with other dealers. We know we have items in our well-known and respected line that will appeal to your trade.

We want to supply you with items that turn over **(b)** rapidly. It does us no good to put goods on your shelves which stay there. When your inventory moves — our inventory moves!

Sincerely,

Alternate Wording:

(a) We will make an adjustment, take back the slow-moving line and replace it with a part of our line you agree should definitely appeal to your particular customers.

(b) Your market is important to us and we want to establish a working relationship that will last for years. We realize that we do not do satisfactory business in a market unless we are concerned with matching the goods and the promotions to the market. We only sell when our goods move at retail.

Model Letter 12-2

Dear _____:

I appreciate your bringing the problem with our components to my attention. I appreciate your concern because of the importance of this component to your reputation for quality. As we discussed by telephone, here is what we know about the problem and what we will do to correct it.

You indicate the shear pin provided on the gear component is shearing at loads below that provided in the contract specifications. As a result you are receiving excessive customer complaints and service problems.

I have instructed our service engineer to call on you   **(a)**
within the next two days to gather samples of the shear pins provided and to run tests on them. In addition, he is to work with your engineers to determine the adequacy of the shear load provided in the specifications with the possibility of increasing it if necessary.

Our aim is to solve the problem to your satisfaction as soon as possible. I will be checking with our engineer and with you after his call to confirm that you are satisfied.

Sincerely,

Alternate Wording:

(a) Our sales representative will call on you within the next two days to gather samples for our engineers to test. Within a week he will return with one of our best engineers to discuss the findings and to provide any modifications necessary.

There are times when the sales manager may not fully understand the nature of the complaint and finds it impossible to telephone the customer to learn the details. This letter was written to request more information.

Model Letter 12-3

Dear _____:

Thank you for writing me concerning your problem with your door. We appreciate you giving us the opportunity to correct the situation because satisfied customers are the basis of our business. We are proud of our reputation as the manufacturer of the highest quality products in the industry. Please provide me with just a bit more information as quickly as possible so that we can provide satisfaction. Here's what I need to know:

- The model number (should be stamped on a plate in the upper right corner).
- Name of the installing dealer (if you don't know I'll assign a nearby dealer I think highly of to adjust this for us).
- The name of the brand of opener installed.

As soon as I receive this information I'll have our Regional Manager contact our dealer and arrange for them to make whatever adjustments or repairs are necessary. I apologize for your inconvenience and ask you to let your neighbors and friends know that not only do we build a quality product but we stand behind it.

Sincerely,

Some "product complaints" are really about late delivery. If you are in a seasonal industry or have one particularly busy month or quarter you've dealt with this.

Model Letter 12-4

Dear _____:

Your District Representative, Don Hinton, called me today regarding your order.

I traced it through manufacturing and shipping and **(a)** found our shipping department sent it UPS on January 23rd. This means you should be receiving your order as I write this note on January 29th. I'm sure Don will have relayed this information long before you receive this note.

I want to apologize for any inconvenience due to late delivery. We are in a peculiar business because 98% of our orders go out perfect, accurate, and on time. However, there really is no margin for error, we really must reach the point where we have "zero defects." If your order is in the 2% which have some flaw or does not arrive on time, you are not impressed by our 98% perfect record. We are very aware of that and everyone at _____ Co. believes our customers have a right to expect zero defects and we are all striving to reach that goal.

Please allow us to make up for the slip-up and late   **(b)**
delivery by "showing off" our real capability on your next order.

We appreciate your business.

Sincerely,

Alternate Wording:

(a) I traced your order. I found it in the plant and have our best expediter watching over it. It will be sent to the loading dock approximately 10 a.m. tomorrow. They'll get it out to you UPS Next Day Service, which means you'll have your order before you read this note.

(b) I can't blame you if you question our dependability when you encounter difficulty on your very first order with us. I can provide references from accounts who have never had one problem in 5, 10, 25 years of dealing with us. Please give us a second chance. Allow us to "show off" our real capability on your next order.

2. RESPONDING TO A SERVICE COMPLAINT

Service is often an important ingredient in a company's success and its quality must be vigorously maintained. Complaints are not uncommon since service is susceptible to human error.

This letter was written to an irate consumer dissatisfied with service provided by a dealer on a household appliance.

Model Letter 12-5

Dear _____:

I am sorry to learn of the problems you've experienced with our Model X. I understand how you must feel. When an appliance you use almost daily still isn't working dependably after three service calls it's frustrating. And it's embarrassing to us.

As I understand it, you have had three timers installed during the past 12 months and all have failed. The first time the dealer replaced the timer with no charge for parts or labor. The second time the dealer provided the timer without charge but billed you for a service call. The third time you were charged for both parts and labor. You feel the repairs should have been made without cost because you believe there must be some inherent fault in the product to cause the timers to fail in this way. It is our sincere desire to make sure every customer is satisfied with her purchase. And although our dealer acted in accordance with the terms of our warranty, we will be happy to reimburse you for the cost of the timer and two service calls. Please send me your receipts and we will promptly reimburse you.

In the meantime we are having our District Service **(a)** Manager call on you to completely check out your machine. He will locate the cause of the recurring timer problem and fix the machine to your satisfaction.

I'm sorry this problem has occurred, but I am pleased that we have had the opportunity to correct it. We certainly hope to add your name to our many thousands of satisfied customers.

Sincerely,

Alternate Wording:

(a) When a recurring problem is noted on any model our policy is to make a basic design change and provide modification of earlier models free of charge. We have not had problems on this model and suspect either a relatively minor wiring irregularity or improper installation of the timers. If it is the former our Service Manager will fix it, if it is the latter he will properly install the new timer — and provide in-field training to the dealer's service crew to insure other customers do not repeat your unhappy experience. No matter what our District Service Manager finds, be assured that he will make it right with no cost to you.

Occasionally one of the support groups in a company can, with the best of intentions, cause a wide-reaching customer relations problem. Here is a letter used by a sales manager after the Credit Department sent a form letter to most of the company's customers dunning them for small balances in very strong language. The first letter is a note to the regional Sales Managers informing them of what is being done. The second letter is to the offended customers.

Model Letter 12-6

To: Regional Managers

Subject: Recent Credit Letters

You have reported complaints by your salespeople about a collection letter mistakenly sent to some customers. I told you we had a letter of apology going out. The apology letters are ready to mail. A copy is attached for your information.

It was not logistically possible to carbon copy every affected salesperson. Please reassure your sales reps that the offended customers have received an appropriate apology. They should not lose any customers over this unfortunate incident.

Model Letter 12-7

Dear _____:

I want to apologize for the letter mistakenly sent to you by our Credit Department. It seems the computer is programmed to automatically send certain messages when certain things occur. In this case, our computer skipped several steps.

I believe our invoice to you left out certain freight and/or sales tax charges. We then sent you a collection letter for a small balance. Please accept my apology for this embarrassing slip-up. The people at _____ Co., including the Credit Department, appreciate your business. Please bear with them while they sort out this matter.

Thank you for your understanding and patience. We appreciate your business.

Sincerely,

3. RESPONDING TO A COMPLAINT REGARDING A SALESPERSON

People problems are difficult to resolve. Poor communication, poor human relations, and just plain personality conflicts sometimes create friction that must be properly handled. The solution is not always easy. A personality conflict might be resolved by simply switching the account to another salesperson. But what if the account is not conveniently located for the attention of another salesperson? Communication and human relations problems can sometimes be resolved with proper training, but the process is often slow and complex.

When a complaint occurs involving your salesperson, prompt and personal attention is demanded. The telephone is often the best way to get a full understanding of the problem. The letter is an appropriate means for follow-up and providing understanding of what is agreed to as a solution.

Model Letter 12-8

Dear _____:

After our conversation the other day I can understand why you feel the way you do about our Sales Engineer, Bill Smith. I appreciate you phoning me about the incident rather than discontinuing business with us.

However, I do feel personally responsible for the incident. We certainly don't train our salespeople to argue with customers and insult them. I have not been working with Bill regularly as I should, and his behavior the other day is due to my neglect. As I mentioned to you on the phone, Bill knows our product inside-out. He can also analyze a customer's installation and spot opportunities to cut costs and increase production faster than anyone in the industry. He can be a great asset to his customers when he listens to them and understands their objectives completely. But he has a tendency to lecture people, tell them what to do on the basis of the best engineering method. He needs to slow down and learn all about the customer's operation and then recommend the most effective solution under the circumstances.

(a)

Today I talked to Bill about this tendency. He sees it   **(b)**
as a problem and is willing to work to improve. He
realizes his know-it-all attitude has kept him from
being of real value to customers at times. He and I
have agreed on a schedule for me to work with him
regularly. I'll be coaching him to ask questions and
listen so he can put his engineering analysis talents to
work for our clients. When he calls on you next
month, I believe you'll find he is a new person. I
appreciate your cooperation very much.

Sincerely,

Alternate Wording:

(a) As we agreed on the phone, Bill is undoubtedly one of the most
knowledgeable people in our industry from an engineering
standpoint. However, he does not listen to the customer to
determine the customer's exact requirements. I owe it to Bill,
and especially to his customers, to develop this ability in him so
that his technical expertise can be applied to the customer's
requirements.

(b) Today I talked to Bill about the need to listen to his customers
and he was very receptive. It seems he has been close to
arguments with customers several times. He finds this frustrating, because he really is trying to help his customers cut
costs and increase productivity.

4. RESPONDING TO A PRICE COMPLAINT

Pricing is a frequent source of complaints. Three types are
common. Customers may complain that they have paid more for your
product than they would have for a similar item from your competitor.
Or they may complain about an alleged pricing or billing extension error.
Or you may receive complaints from dealers who feel that insufficient
margin is available to profitably handle your product. A model letter is
provided for each of these circumstances.

Model Letter 12-9

Dear _____:

Thank you for letting us know about your concern
that you were overcharged for the sofa you pur-

chased from us last week. Today we must all be concerned about getting the most value possible for each dollar we spend.

As I understand the situation, you feel you could have gotten essentially the same sofa from (competitor) for about $50 less than you paid for the (brand) you purchased from us. As a result, you would like to either return the sofa or receive a refund in that amount from us.

First, let me assure you that we will do everything possible to make you happy with your purchase. We value you as a customer for your repeated purchases and because we know you will tell your friends and neighbors when you are happy.

Comparing furniture can be confusing. Many qualities may be built into an item that are not readily evident but may add considerably to the expected life and enjoyment of the product. Fabric, spring construction, and frame construction are just three. It is also possible for a manufacturer to produce look-alike products for less by lowering the quality of such materials. The real price the buyer pays is as much as half as long as product life and early wear, which makes the item unsightly within months of purchase.

May I suggest this as a possible solution. Within the next few days come into the store and ask for me. I will be happy to show you the features that are built into the product that will provide more years of useful life than any other line. Then if you still feel the other brand provides the best value, you may return the sofa for full refund.

Fair enough? I will be looking forward to seeing you in the store soon.

Sincerely,

This letter responds to a pricing complaint due to what the customer felt might be a mistake on an invoice.

Model Letter 12-10

Dear _____ :

I appreciate your expressing concern about the price charged for (item) on invoice #xxxx. I know you are willing to pay the worth of the product but not more.

I've checked it personally and believe the billing to be correct. The current price is $xx as was announced in a price adjustment letter on October 1. The extension for the number ordered is also correct. We do make billing errors from time to time despite our care to make sure each invoice is correct. Thanks for keeping us on our toes.

Sincerely,

The following letter was written in response to a dealer who complained of insufficient margin on a product.

Model Letter 12-11

Dear _____ :

I can certainly understand your desire to secure a fair margin on every product you handle. We strive for the same end result.

As we discussed by telephone, our products are generally priced to provide a 30% mark up. As you know, our dealers had been asking for a basic, low-cost model all last year. We have always maintained that quality is what we are known for and that is what your customers want when they ask you for our products. When we finally agreed to offer the basic model we made it clear that we had cut our own margin to a nominal amount and the dealers should understand this product allows them to offer cost-conscious buyers an alternative. This product is not a money-maker. We suggest you continue to sell our main line and use the basic model to keep cost-conscious buyers in your store. You're doing them a big favor when you do sell them our economy model rather than let them go elsewhere for one of the discount products. Our economy model is the equivalent of a Rolls Royce compared to the lower quality goods they would pay the same price for at your competitors.

But do not expect to be able to enjoy the same margin on the economy model that you do on the rest of our line. Thank you for bringing your concern to me. I hope this explanation answers your question concerning our price on the new model. You are a very important dealer and we want to maintain your confidence. If you have any other questions please don't hesitate to phone me next week.

Sincerely,

13

LETTERS THAT OPEN THE DOOR FOR THE SALES CALL

13

LETTERS THAT OPEN THE DOOR FOR THE SALES CALL

The most refined of sales skill is of little value if the sales rep cannot get an appointment with his prospect. In many instances making cold calls on prospects may be a practical means for opening a sales approach with a prospect. More effective for most businesses is to secure an appointment with the prospect through a telephone call or letter. Each has its place. The telephone call is valuable due to its sense of immediacy. And it provides for more accurate determination of the prospect's initial reaction to your request for appointment. The letter avoids the problem of reaching the prospect at an inopportune time. It affords the opportunity for presenting credentials. And it can often be combined with the follow-up telephone call to make a very effective appointment-making combination.

A letter seeking an appointment is a miniature sales call. As such it involves three elements. First, it must provide some potential benefit to the prospect for granting the interview you request. Second, it must briefly review the facts that will assist the prospect to make an evaluation of what you ask. And third, it should propose the next step — the action you seek. In many instances, the next step sought by the letter is a follow-up telephone call for an appointment. Many of the letters in this chapter could be sent by the sales manager or could be used directly by the sales rep. You might also consider going through the letters in this chapter and selecting those you believe your sales force could use most effectively. You could make any minor revisions necessary to tailor them to your market and then introduce them at a sales meeting. At that time you would explain the letters, identify the unique purpose of each, and explain how to use the letters most effectively as part of a total sales approach.

1. SEEKING APPOINTMENT WITH NO PREVIOUS CONTACTS

Perhaps the most difficult appointment to secure is where no previous contact has been made with the prospect and where no mutual acquaintance or interest is available to serve as an opener. So let's tackle that one first. This letter could be sent by the sales manager or by the sales rep. It sets up a telephone call to follow shortly after the letter.

Model Letter 13-1

Dear _____:

If you are like most busy executives, you can always squeeze in time to keep abreast of the latest developments and ideas in semiconductor engineering.

My schedule brings me to your city on (date). I would **(a)** appreciate an opportunity to meet with you at your convenience to share some ideas which may be useful to you.

I shall telephone you in a few days to make an **(b)** appointment.

Sincerely,

Alternate Wording:

(a) I believe I have some new ideas to share which may be useful to you.

(b) I will arrive in your city Monday and will count on meeting with you for lunch if that is convenient for you. I'll telephone you Thursday to confirm our meeting.

Here is another letter designed to accomplish the same purpose. This one is longer but is just as powerful.

Model Letter 13-2

Dear _____:

Communication is one of the vital keys to modern marketing in today's highly competitive business society. Executives spend sleepless nights mulling over "people problems" because it takes emotional and unpredictable people to produce and sell products and services to equally emotional and unpredictable customers.

The problems of communicating are tremendous, and yet we are in an age of technological explosion wherein the changes portending in the next ten years stagger the imagination. Our services can help you SOLVE YOUR COMMUNICATION PROBLEMS — *BOTH EXTERNAL AND INTERNAL.*

We are staffed and geared to take on an entire **(a)** assignment . . . analysis, planning, creating, staging . . . with printed materials, incentive programs, motion pictures, slides, filmstrips, video . . . multi-media shows, exhibits . . . everything you need to achieve your objectives.

Recent projects include (select some recent programs that would be of interest to the prospect).

Enclosed are our company brochure and other printed materials which will give you details on the scope, dimension, and professionalism of the _____ organization.

May I have an opportunity to meet with you and show you examples of our work? Unless I hear from you sooner, I plan to contact you in a few days to set up an appointment.

Sincerely,

Alternate Wording:

(a) Our list of satisfied clients reads like *Fortune's* list of top-ranking U.S. Corporations but also includes many smaller companies interested in growing and increasing profits. Our motion picture and video productions have won over 150 awards for excellence at film festivals all over the world. Our three convenient studio locations mean your job can be done where it should be done with dispatch and economy.

This letter provides a novel approach.

Model Letter 13-3

Dear _____ :

Are you besieged with solicitations about premium ideas and new ideas to save and make you money? Where do most of them end up — in your waste basket?

STOP!! Don't throw this letter away! Reading the next paragraph could improve your company profit.

We are professional problem-solvers. The enclosed Fact Sheet describes just one problem we solved for (Name of customer).

We would like to include _____ as one of our satisfied clients. When can we get together and tap our know-how and experience on your behalf? Increased sales and profits become mutual goals when we join forces.

We'll come to you. No obligation. Just say when!

Sincerely,

The above letter is one of a series that is sent to a prospect. Here is another in the series. When two or three letters of this type have been sent to the prospect, the sales rep calls for an appointment.

Model Letter 13-4

Dear _____ :

Does the name (name of your company) ring a bell?
We solve problems!

The enclosed fact sheet reveals another marketing problem solved for (name of client).

What is your biggest hang-up? We want to put our collective brains to work on it — why not challenge us? We guarantee results.

Just pick up your phone and dial _____ — you'll get attention.

Sincerely,

2. SEEKING APPOINTMENT BASED ON A REFERRAL

A referral provides a solid basis for securing a first call appointment. Customers, friends, suppliers all provide a mutual point-of-reference to get receptivity. In addition, references provide a low-key sense of obligation — not an obligation to buy, but at least to provide the courtesy of attention.

Model Letter 13-5

Dear _____:

Interested in reducing your packaging costs by as much as 10%? That's what Bill Johnson at Acme Manufacturing was able to accomplish.

As a direct result of his excellent savings achievement, he would like to share the same possibility with some of his friends. So he happily consented for me to write this letter. **(a)**

I will be in the Chicago area on Tuesday, February 6. I would be happy to explain in detail how Bill was able to achieve such significant cost reductions. Interested? I'll call you this week to setup an appointment. **(b)**

Sincerely,

Alternate Wording:

(a) Bill believes the simple, common-sense approach we take to packaging may be interesting to you and was happy to allow me to mention his satisfaction to you.

(b) Interested in how such cost reductions can be achieved? I will phone you this week to set up an appointment for Tuesday, February 6 or Wednesday, February 7.

This letter was written by a retail furniture sales manager as a result of a lead from one of his customers.

Model Letter 13-6

Dear _____:

When you locate a store that really cares about you and goes out of its way to make you a satisfied customer, you want to tell the world. And that's just what is happening with Mrs. Jane Meyers. She has been so pleased with her recent purchases at _____ that she wants you to know.

Mrs. Meyers' experience is not all that unusual around here. As a matter of fact we usually succeed in getting that type of enthusiastic endorsement from our customers.

Give us a try. You, too, may want to do a little shouting about your satisfaction with _____.

Sincerely,

3. LETTERS OF REPLY TO UNSOLICITED REQUESTS FOR INFORMATION

Depending on the type of product or service you sell, prospects may come to you seeking information about your product. The customer is most likely to take the initiative in response to advertising or conversations with customers. Occasionally, prospects may write to inquire if you can fill a particular need. This type of unique sales opportunity calls for a well-written sales letter. Here are several.

Model Letter 13-7

Dear _____:

Here is the _____ literature you requested.   **(a)**
We have tried to make the information provided there as complete as possible. But we have not been able to tailor the application of the product to your specific situation. Only a personal meeting can do that.

When you have had a chance to read the literature   **(b)**
and to determine if the _____ line seems to fit

your needs, I will have our sales rep, Ms. _____, call you for an appointment. In that way she will be able to provide you with the information you need to determine *exactly* what you might expect in the way of performance and precisely which model will best fit your needs.

I'll have her call you on Thursday.

Sincerely,

Alternate Wording:

(a) Thank you for your request for additional information and literature. I was not completely sure which model and what optional equipment would fit your needs and did not wish to send information which did not apply.

(b) I have asked our representative, Ms. _____, to call on you so that you may determine exactly what you might expect in the way of performance and precisely which model will best fit your needs.

Perhaps you use your advertising program as a source of sales leads. Many companies use a coupon in their ads to solicit inquiries. In addition, some prospects may write letters of inquiry concerning some ad they have seen. This letter was written replying to such an inquiry.

Model Letter 13-8

Dear _____ :

We are pleased that you have asked for particulars concerning our _____ line as advertised in the December issue of _____ Additional information is enclosed.

We have been featuring the _____ line for the past several months in the _____ *Journal* because of its unique application to your type of business. In fact we now have over 140 customers using the _____ line in applications similar to yours.

Since you may have questions remaining even after you have read the enclosed literature, I have asked our representative, _____, to call you some time in the next few days.

Thanks for your interest in the _____.

Sincerely,

This letter was written in response to a prospect who wrote to the company inquiring if it had a product to fill a particular need.

Model Letter 13-9

Dear _____:

Thank you for thinking of _____ to fill your needs. We manufacture 32 different models of valves that might fit the application you describe. So surely at least one of them will do the job precisely.

I have asked our sales representative, _____, to call you in the next few days. With a better idea of your application, he will be able to recommend the particular valve to meet your requirements.

We appreciate the opportunity to be of service and look forward to assisting you further.

Sincerely,

Perhaps you have sent literature to a prospect as requested and now need a follow-up. This letter is designed to jog such a prospect into action.

Model Letter 13-10

Dear _____:

Have you ever thrown a rock over a cliff and listened for it to hit the water? If you didn't hear it splash you would, no doubt, wonder what had happened. Well, this is the position I'm in on your inquiry regarding our equipment. I'm anxious to know whether my handling of your request was satisfactory.

While it's not our desire to waste your time with needless and bothersome solicitation, I'm wondering if we may be of any further service. We welcome the opportunity to answer any questions you may have and will try to provide practical solutions for your particular application.

With my letter I am enclosing several questions and

their answers which we find most commonly asked
by those considering the purchase of our equipment.

I look forward to hearing from you.

Sincerely,

4. LETTER TO TRADE SHOW REGISTRANTS

Another valuable source for prospect leads may be trade shows,
fairs, etc. which provide the opportunity to display your products to
potential buyers. Many marketers offer registration opportunities at
their display booths in return for prizes or other incentives. The prospect
registration provides an expanded mailing list that should be quickly
followed up with a letter and a sales visit if warranted.

Here is a letter that provides a good follow-up to a trade show
registration.

Model Letter 13-11

Dear _____:

Thank you for visiting our booth at the Housewares
Show. As you saw, we have many products that offer
outstanding merchandising and profit opportunities.
For example, you may have seen (two or three
products) — just to name a few.

Enclosed are catalog pages and prices for the coming   **(a)**
product season. In addition, we provide an attractive
discount program and frequent incentives.

Our products will be supported by an intensive
advertising program right in your local area.

We would like to consider you as a proud dealer of
_____ products. Our sales representative will be
in contact with you in the next week or two to
answer any questions you might have.

Sincerely,

Alternate Wording:

(a) We hope these products interested you. We would like to have
the opportunity to discuss some additional advantages of our
product such as an attractive discount program and intensive
advertising.

5. "THANK YOU" FOR COURTESIES SHOWN OUR SALES REP

Follow-up after the sales rep's first call is important for two reasons. A follow-up letter provides the opportunity to put your company's name before the prospect one more time to better fix its image in his mind. In addition, a follow-up letter provides a necessary demonstration of appreciation for the prospect's hospitality. The following letters provide a sound basis for follow-up.

Model Letter 13-12

Dear _____:

I enjoyed our meeting yesterday and I appreciate it.

As you review our proposal, I hope you will consider carefully two very important benefits your company will enjoy:

1. You will be able to reduce your payroll preparation costs by as much as $8,500 per year;

2. You will be able to quickly receive the cost analysis reports you require to effectively control your business. These reports will be provided with no time required by you or your people.

Enclosed is the booklet I promised. Notice on page   **(a)**
three the experience related by one of our customers. You will find their comments are rather typical of the results to be expected from our automated payroll service.

I will call you later this week to discuss your reaction to the program.

Sincerely,

Alternate Wording:

(a) Enclosed is the booklet I promised. I have also attached the names of several customers whose circumstances are similar to yours. These companies have received the benefits which we discussed. You may be interested in talking with them.

Model Letter 13-13

Dear _____:

Thank you for the opportunity to meet with you at your office. The time you took from your busy schedule to spend with me was both enjoyable and rewarding. I trust it was beneficial to you as well. Your thoughts provided me a much clearer picture of your firm's operations.

Please give some thought to the various services we discussed and we'll be looking forward to the possibility of working with you on any projects you may be planning within our area of specialty. **(a)**

I shall make it a point to keep in touch and hope you will not hesitate to call us should you desire further information or assistance on a specific project.

Sincerely,

Alternate Wording:

(a) I believe several of the services we discussed may have application to your foundry. I would be happy to develop a proposal on any one or more that may be of specific interest to you.

14

LETTERS THAT RESOLVE DIFFICULT CREDIT PROBLEMS

14

LETTERS THAT RESOLVE
DIFFICULT CREDIT
PROBLEMS

When delinquent accounts are ignored, they become more diffi-cult to collect without losing a customer.

Some organizations expect the sales force to collect delinquent accounts in the early stages, but transfer responsibility to the Credit Department at some agreed-upon point, for instance 60 or 90 days past due. Other companies are rigidly departmentalized and the sales manager would rarely be involved in prompting payment from accounts. And other companies hold the Sales Department totally responsible for collections. No matter which approach your company follows, some of the letters in this chapter will be valuable to you.

A large part of your sales management job is to keep your sales force selling at peak efficiency, and one facet of that job is to structure the sales function to emphasize productive direct selling activities. Some non-sales activities must be tolerated as a necessary evil in most sales jobs; however, non-sales-producing activities should be minimized. One responsibility which may be included in the sales job is the collection of overdue accounts.

For most salespeople this is a difficult and distasteful task. They can spend an inordinate amount of time and effort worrying about stimulating slow-paying accounts and as a result sales may suffer. Use of these letters can avoid that consequence.

The salesperson should know about all correspondence with the customer before it is sent to the customer. In some sales organizations this requires coordination with the Credit Department. In some cases, letters stimulating payment from overdue accounts originate from the line sales manager. In these cases the salesperson should receive a copy of the correspondence before it is sent to the customer and the letter should smooth the way for the sales rep's call.

1. DECLINING A REQUEST FOR SPECIAL TERMS

Occasionally customers will ask your salespeople for preferential credit terms which they do not have the authority to grant. The rep then brings the request to the sales manager. Particularly if a large account is involved, the sales representative may make a strong pitch for granting the customer's request. The sales manager may consider the request or, if necessary, take it up with the appropriate authority in the company. When the decision is against granting the request, the sales manager has to reply without demoralizing the salesperson or losing a customer.

Model Letter 14-1

Dear _____:

I've discussed the _____ Company's request for an additional cash discount with the proper people at headquarters. Because of the size and prestige of this account, I went as high as the Director of Finance. The answer is a definite "no." Let me explain why.

We have had similar requests for special terms — which amount to a lower price or a discount — from several large accounts recently. The company has tactfully denied each of these requests, without noting any decline in business from these companies, by the way. Our company position is, if we grant one such request our other key accounts will expect the same. We would then either cave in to all their requests and have lower margins or lose some big accounts.

As we discussed this, I found myself thinking specifically about three more key accounts in your territory. If we were to grant this discount to _____ Company, how long do you think it would take those three to demand the same thing? And you know you'd end up losing business and maybe losing a couple of major accounts completely. No, the more I thought about it, the clearer it became that we're way ahead in the long run to sell _____ Company on being happy with their current terms. If you and I could make the decision without Finance's involvement, I think we'd decide to deny this request ourselves.

I've enclosed a copy of the letter I've prepared to send them. Call me tomorrow to discuss and coordinate.

Sincerely,

Model Letter 14-2

Dear _____ :

Bill brought your request for cash discount terms to me and he and I have explored the possibility with the appropriate people in our company. Bill and I received a short college course in pricing from our Credit and Accounting people in the process, by the way.

As you know, our products are priced as low as **(a)** anyone in the industry. From your Accounting Department's standpoint, the credit terms offered to the market are as much a cost of the product as assembly or machining or any other production cost. Their answer to me was that any cost savings they can make in the future will be passed on to the customer. But right now the price of our product is as low as possible without sacrificing the quality you must have.

So, for the present, I must tell you that it is not possible to offer cash discount terms.

Bill will be in to see you next week to discuss an innovative product which may help lower your costs, and he will be glad to answer any other questions you may have at that time.

Sincerely,

Alternate Wording:

(a) Without "passing the buck" to our Credit Department, let me pass on the explanation they gave me. Since cash discount terms are a discount for prompt payment, those terms are usually taken into consideration when products are priced. Our company's policy has been to price our products as low as possible to begin with. So, from our Accounting Department's point of view, the cash discount is being given to our customers in advance.

2. PROMPTING AN ACCOUNT AT FIRST SIGN OF SLOWNESS IN PAYMENT

Many companies have a policy to follow when an account does not pay within agreed terms. Usually a series of communication steps are provided for central use in the Credit Department or for decentralized use in the field. Generally, a friendly reminder when the account first goes past due is productive in several ways. It serves as a "temperature take" to find out if you have a collection problem. The invoice may simply have been misplaced and the friendly reminder brings it to the account's attention and urges payment with no loss of good will. The customer may have some questions about the bill and the reminder will prompt him or her to call and get the answers. The account may not have been satisfied with the product or service and the letter will prompt the customer to bring the grievance out in the open so the sales rep can deal with it. This letter should be simply a reminder, and it should assume that the customer is satisfied, intended to pay within the agreed terms, but may have simply overlooked or misplaced the invoice.

Model Letter 14-3

Dear _____ :

I received a call from our Credit Department today asking about your account. You have paid within the discount terms for as long as I've been manager of this Region, and I'm sure for a long while before that.

I suspect our last invoice simply was misplaced in your Accounting Department. If there has been any problem with the billing or with our product or service please let me know. Otherwise, I assume there was a slip-up and we'll be back to giving you your discount again next month.

Sincerely,

Model Letter 14-4

Dear _____ :

The last few days have been hectic. When I cleaned **(a)** out my "IN" basket this morning I found several invoices from suppliers dangerously close to past due.

I suspect you've been in a similar situation recently and our invoice #XXXX dated March 1, 19XX is on the bottom of your "IN" basket, on your secretary's desk, or lost in the Accounting Department.

Just put it through for payment — or when Bob calls on you next week, tell him to bill you again if the original invoice hasn't turned up.

Sincerely,

Alternate Wording:

(a) Several invoices were already past the due date. Next I looked over the invoices sent to our customers 60 days ago and noticed one sent to you.

Model Letter 14-5

Dear _____ :

I was reviewing last month's shipments this morning, and, seeing several orders from you, was reminded again of the ideal working relationship we have. I appreciate the business we receive from you and wanted to remind you that I am here if I can be of service in any way.

I know your sales have been increasing and it is good to see you having such a great year. Would you take a minute to check on a couple of invoices for me? My records show invoices _____ and _____ unpaid from last month. Just send them through for payment when they appear, or let Bob know if there is any problem with them when he calls on you next week.

Thanks again,

3. PROMPTING AN ACCOUNT A SECOND TIME WHEN SLOWNESS PERSISTS

When the first friendly reminder brings no response it is time for a more direct approach. In some companies this may be the point where the Credit Department, bookkeeper, or Chief Financial Officer takes over. The account is probably 60 to 90 days past due at this point. If you are still the correspondent but will have to turn it over to Credit or Accounting if payment isn't made after this round, you may want to carbon copy the department which will succeed you.

Model Letter 14-6

Dear _____:

I've asked Nancy to discuss invoice #XXXX with you when she calls on you next week. I've asked her to bring a check back so that we can be sure of providing you uninterrupted service. Your account is dangerously close to the automatic cutoff point where deliveries are stopped until our Credit Manager has contacted you and received payment.

If you have any disagreement with the invoice please contact Nancy or me immediately so that we can clear the matter up and continue to serve you without interruption.

Sincerely,

Model Letter 14-7

Dear _____:

We discussed invoices _____ and _____ last month and determined that they were accurate. It was my understanding that you would send payment shortly. Phil will be calling on you next Wednesday. Perhaps the most practical way to clear these invoices would be to pull them out of the normal accounting routine and hand Phil a check when he comes in Wednesday.   **(a)**

I'll be talking to him by phone on Friday, and I'll remind him to ask you for a check and give you a paid receipt when he visits you.

Sincerely,

Alternate Wording:

(a) I know invoices can get lost in the shuffle of daily bookkeeping. So, may I suggest you pull these invoices out of your normal accounting routine and hand Phil a check this Wednesday.

4. INFORMING CUSTOMERS THAT YOUR INTERNAL CREDIT DEPARTMENT WILL BE CONTACTING THEM

Some companies have a policy of turning correspondence over to the Credit Department when the Sales Department has not been able to obtain prompt payment within a certain time (usually 60 to 90 days). Informing the customer that the Credit Department is taking over can give the sales manager one more chance to collect amicably.

Model Letter 14-8

Dear _____:

When we talked on the telephone two weeks ago I thought we had an agreement. My understanding was that you had no disagreement with our invoice #XXXX and intended to send payment immediately. I have been watching the mail and have your next order on the shipping dock ready to go as soon as your account is current.

This Friday your account goes over the limit set by   **(a)**
our company policy for me to deal with and is officially turned over to our Credit Department. Your sales representative will stop by Thursday. We can continue to work together on open account if you

clear this up Thursday. Please phone me immediately if you have any problem with this arrangement.

Sincerely,

Alternate Wording:

(a) Your company has been on our preferred customer list for years, meaning we have filled your orders in time of shortage, granted special terms on occasion when you had a large job in progress, granted special quantity discounts. We have delivered on short notice when you were in a bind. In short, we have been a good supplier. This Friday your account reaches the past due point where our Credit Department takes over. This would put you on a cash only basis after years of enjoying the advantage of preferred credit.

Model Letter 14-9

Dear _____:

We have discussed your outstanding balance several **(a)** times in the last two months. I believe we agree that our product is most suitable to your production methods and we wish to continue as your supplier.

The amount and age of your outstanding invoices force me to turn over correspondence on this matter to our Credit Manager at the end of this month unless payment is received before that date.

I will phone you this Friday to discuss payment. I want to continue to serve you on open account, and I believe you see advantages to your company in continuing to deal with us on open account.

Let's clear this matter up on Friday.

Sincerely,

5. PLACING AN ACCOUNT ON C.O.D.

Occasionally your Credit Department will accept orders on a cash only basis from a particular account. If you make your own credit decisions, you may also come to the conclusion that a particular account should be sold on a cash basis because of past payment record, weak financial condition, or another valid reason.

This is a difficult letter to write. Remember you are still selling, the terms are a part of the total package of values the customer is buying, and unfavorable terms may outweigh the other advantages of your product or service and lose the sale.

This letter was written by a sales manager who could not extend open account terms, but wanted the business enough to sell the customer on the advantages of buying on a cash basis.

Model Letter 14-10

Dear _____:

I want to thank you for your order of January 15th. The advantage of our plating method goes further than just lower initial cost. The superior durability will be an attractive plus to your customers and will give your sales force the edge in a competitive market.

We will ship your order on a cash basis and of course you will receive our cash discount further lowering your cost.

We value your business and hope that you agree with the cost and quality advantages of this arrangement.

Sincerely,

6. INFORMING A CUSTOMER THAT THE ACCOUNT IS BEING TURNED OVER TO COLLECTORS

You occasionally reach the point where there is no alternative but to turn an account over to an outside collection agency. Don't feel too badly, the law of averages dictates that you can't win them all. You will already have been diplomatic, subtle, and friendly in a first reminder letter. Firm and businesslike, pointing out the advantages of open account, was the tone of later letters. The strategy in second and even third and fourth letters is usually to retain an active account as well as collect what is past due. Finally, you are to the point of not wanting future business from the account — you just want your money.

Model Letter 14-11

Dear _____:

We have written you numerous times regarding **(a)**
your substantial past due balance. You have not

responded to our requests for payment. Your failure to comply forces us to turn your account over to _____ agency for collection. A representative of that firm will contact you after a ten-day grace period.

We urge you to take advantage of this grace period to avoid litigation, preserve your credit rating, and avoid additional legal costs.   **(b)**

Sincerely,

Alternate Wording:

(a) You have ignored our previous requests for payment of your past due account. Do not force us to take more direct action.

(b) If we do not receive payment within ten days our attorney will become responsible for collecting the amount due.

Model Letter 14-12

Dear _____:

It seldom becomes necessary for us to turn an account over to an attorney for collection. And on those few occasions when circumstances leave us no alternative, we consider it only fair to tell the customer exactly what we intend to do.

Certainly you realize that we have made every effort   **(a)**
to be fair and patient in requesting you to settle your account of $_____.

We have written to you several times, asking that you let us know how we could cooperate with you in getting this indebtedness straightened out. Your continued silence leaves us no alternative but reluc-   **(b)**
tantly to refer your account to our Attorney for collection. So, won't you respond to this final appeal for your cooperation and avoid a procedure that can only mean additional expense to you?

Unless we hear from you within five days we shall be compelled to transfer your account to the office of our attorney.

Very truly yours

Alternate Wording:

(a) We have been most patient in awaiting payment of your long overdue obligation. However, despite our sincere spirit of cooperation, we have had no word or check from you in answer to our request.

(b) We must now insist that payment be forwarded at once. If we do not receive your check in ten days, your account will be turned over to our attorney.

7. ENCOURAGING CUSTOMERS TO TAKE DISCOUNTS

Cash flow is an important part of the business plan of most growing companies. Money tied up in accounts receivable could be used to produce more inventory to support the sales force in increasing sales. Of course, accounts receivable will also have to go up as volume increases, but faster collection of receivables is almost always a goal of growth organizations. And customers may increase their purchases as the per-unit cost decreases, and taking cash discounts reduces the per-unit cost.

Model Letter 14-13

Dear _____:

Would you be interested in increasing your profit margin on our products at retail by 2%? We are proud of the substantial margin our dealers earn on our products. In looking over the orders you have placed over the past six months, I believe there is an opportunity for you to further increase your profits on our merchandise.

We offer 2/10/Net 30 terms, a real opportunity for additional profits which is easily overlooked. Try it on your next order — I think you'll like that extra 2%.

Sincerely

Model Letter 14-14

Dear _____:

Thank you for the order you placed January 16. I noted that this was the second order you have placed for this new type of bushing and asked Tom about it. He told me how you have found a way to simplify an assembly operation and thereby reduce labor cost by using this bushing. I'm glad we can help as you continue to find ways to reduce costs while increasing quality in a competitive industry.

I know this is important to you and believe I can suggest a way to reduce costs even further. We offer 2/10/Net 30 terms and you have always been very prompt to pay — 30 days or less. I suspect you could have payment sent in ten days just as easily and take the 2% discount. Our company recently checked our own accounts payable accounting methods and found we were missing discount terms by just a few days in many cases. Tom will check with you on his next call to see if this is practical with your accounting methods. We want to assist you in maintaining quality and reducing costs in every way we can.

Sincerely,

8. USING CREDIT MESSAGES TO INVITE ADDITIONAL PURCHASES FROM YOUR BEST CUSTOMERS

Whether you deal with consumers, retailers, wholesalers, or industrial customers, you can use credit messages to invite additional purchases from your best customers. You may want to use special V.I.P. identification cards or numbers. You may wish to have your credit manager send out your message rather than have it come from the Sales Department. You may wish to use mailgrams to add weight to your message. Whatever devices you use the message should clearly say, "You're a very important customer. Your credit is good with us. We want to be sure you get extra-special treatment."

Model Letter 14-15

Dear _____:

The purpose of this letter is to confirm the excellent status of your credit account.

Because our Credit Department appreciates the splendid manner in which you have done business with us in the past, we consider it a privilege to issue you the special V.I.P. card enclosed. Use this card or the V.I.P. number, and it will identify you to all of our credit, sales, and service personnel as a very special person. It is a pleasure to do business with you.

Sincerely,

15

SPECIAL-EVENT INVITATIONS THAT GET ACTION

15

SPECIAL-EVENT INVITATIONS THAT GET ACTION

For many businesses trade shows, dealer meetings, and plant tours provide an important method for building sales. Your business may invest thousands of dollars in such events each year. But if the prospect or customer fails to attend the function or misses your booth, the investment is lost. Convincing the prospect and customers to participate in such events is as much a sales job as convincing them to buy your product or service. To visit your display booth at a trade show may require little or no cash outlay, but it does require time — valuable time that may be worth as much or more to the prospect.

The letter is a valuable tool for getting the customer's commitment to act on your invitation. The letter can be a personalized sales tool. It can sell for some time as it lingers on the prospect's desk nudging one to action. When it is combined with a personal phone call, a letter can provide a one-two punch that can often move the most difficult of prospects to action.

You may want to seek some form of commitment from the prospect to attend a trade show or other sales function. It is best if the commitment is in writing. Even that may not be enough. Those who have had experience with getting prospects and customers to follow through on their commitments to attend sales functions know how difficult it is to get action without frequent prodding. You might initially ask for the return of a postcard or a telephone call to indicate that the customer will attend. Subsequently you might want to send a last-minute reminder of the event and the customer's commitment. Also in order would be another telephone call a day or two before the event to confirm the customer will be there. In some instances it might be necessary to pick up a customer or prospect. Whatever it takes, the letter is an excellent first step to getting commitment.

1. LETTERS TO URGE CUSTOMERS TO ATTEND A TRADE SHOW

The trade show is a time-established method for introducing new models, for informing buyers of new marketing trends and for stirring new enthusiasm into customer marketing organizations. It is an important and busy time of year for many marketers. This is an excellent time for cementing relationships with established customers. It provides an opportunity for salespeople to talk with customers, to make sales, to establish a company image of progressiveness. Even if your customers do not come to the trade show, they should be aware that you will. That provides a reinforced impression of your company as an aggressive merchandiser.

You may want to send out letters to customers that are somewhat different from those to prospects. The following model letters are designed for your customer base.

Model Letter 15-1

Dear _____ :

It's one of the biggest events of the year in the _____ industry. And (your company) will be an important part of it. I'm speaking of the Trade Show coming up on (date) at (place).

I know you have gone to the trade show in the past and I hope you are planning to take part this year. There are a number of important reasons that you should:

1. Ours is a constantly changing industry. The annual trade show provides a quick and reliable way to keep abreast of new products and opening markets.

2. The trade show provides a means for you to get your orders placed early and while product is readily available.

3. The trade show committee has done an excellent job of providing seminars to help us all broaden our understanding of the industry and the changes that are occurring in it. These are probably a must for you as they are for a good share of those in attendance.

4. The trade show provides an opportunity to meet and share ideas with your competitors in the industry. It's always a good idea to keep in touch, to determine what they are doing that's new and challenging.

5. The trade show provides an opportunity to get away and reflect. As with most of us, it is probably hard to tear yourself away from the press of business. But once it's done you will probably be able to return with renewed vigor and a basket of new ideas for strengthening your business.

_____ will be at booth _____. Be sure to look **(a)** us up. I have made sure that a little gift is set aside there for you. Just make yourself known to the representative on duty. And while you're there, be sure to check out our new line of _____ Not only do we feel it will beat out anything else in the show, we are making available a trade show special you won't want to miss.

I'm looking forward to seeing you at the show.

Sincerely,

Alternate Wording:

(a) If you will be attending, return the enclosed postcard. I'll make sure there is an attractive gift set aside at our booth for you.

Model Letter 15-2

Dear _____:

Yes, we'll be at the 19___ _____ Trade Show. And we hope we'll see you there. Last year 87% of our customers made it to the show and stopped by our booth.

The _____ Trade Show is an important event for our customers and for us. At this year's show we will be featuring three new product lines you will want to be sure to see. Each one provides a substantial profit potential. In addition we will be introducing our new and improved polystructural product line which in stress tests shows 35% greater strength and a much reduced failure rate.

And that's not all. We'll be introducing a brand-new sales aid . . . a new video tape demonstrating the installation of our PVC low-pressure valve line. You'll find it an important counter and sales rep aid that will make selling easy and profitable.

We'll be at booths 123 and 125 this year. Our display is new and expanded. Be sure to look us up.

Sincerely,

Model Letter 15-3

Dear _____:

Don't Miss the _____ Trade Show!

Our display is bigger and better than ever this year. **(a)** And we'll be giving away prizes every hour just for registering.

I've enclosed a floor plan map with an X showing where we will be located.

It is the most important three days you can invest all year. We'll look for you there.

Sincerely,

Alternate Wording:

(a) If you'll be attending the trade show, return the enclosed postcard. Then drop by and register at the booth. Your early return of the postcard will double your chances of winning in the hour you register.

2. LETTERS TO ENCOURAGE PROSPECTS TO SEEK OUT YOUR TRADE SHOW BOOTH

For many companies, the annual trade show is a most important event for identifying new prospects and for developing their interest in your products and company. But even though you spend thousands on a display, it will be of little value if your prospects do not visit it. A good letter will set your prospects up so they will seek you out during the show.

Model Letter 15-4

Dear _____:

VISIT THE _____ TRADE SHOW!

Why? It's the one big opportunity that all distributors have for examining new lines, becoming familiar with suppliers, keeping in touch with what's happening in our ever-changing business.

If you're considering broadening your line, be sure to check us out. You'll find our display of 47 (type of product) items at (booth location).

We have some top potential areas open and we're looking for the best distributors in the business to fill them. If you qualify, you will be joining a growing organization that offers a top quality product supported with excellent advertising, sales promotion, and sales help.

Look us up at the trade show. We'll be happy to take the time to prove to you that a move to _____ can be your best marketing decision all year.

Sincerely,

Model Letter 15-5

_____(Company Name)_____

invites you to

A MANAGEMENT PREVIEW
OF NEWEST MARKING
AND LABELING SYSTEMS

Time to re-evaluate your labeling and marking?

Please join us at 1:30 p.m.

To hear . . .

Learn the newest techniques and ideas for getting the most from your marking and labeling systems. Find out how others are using our systems to get more done at less cost.

DATE:

April 23, 19___

TIME:

1:30 p.m. only

PLACE:

Holiday Inn — Room C
Exit 12 — Marine Turnpike

TRAVELING TRADE SHOW | Response Card

(Company Name)
_____

☐　　Count on me. I'll be there.

☐　　Sorry. I can't make it this time.

_____
Name　　　　　Title

_____
Name　　　　　Title

_____
Company

_____
Address

_____
Telephone

Model Letter 15-6

Dear _____:

Industry experts are predicting that more than (number of units) of the rapidly growing (name of line) will be sold in the coming year. That's a sizeable market. If you're considering getting in on the action but haven't yet decided on the best company and brand to go with, be sure to stop by our display at the _____ Show at McCormick Place next month.

You'll find 21 models on display, the most extensive in the industry. You'll also find a complete display of our advertising and sales promotion programs. A knowledgeable (name of company) representative will be on hand to explain our dealer program and to answer your questions.

You might want to visit our booth first. That way you'll have a good comparison to use as you take in the other displays at the show.

Bring this letter along and present it to one of the   **(a)**
representatives at our display. It will help to identify
you as a special visitor. And for that we will be happy
to give you a copy of the book "_____" just as our
way of saying thanks for stopping by.

Sincerely,

Alternate Wording:

(a) Just in hope of getting to know you better, we are holding a
hospitality hour each evening of the trade show. Drop by,
won't you, any evening from 7 through 10:30. Just bring this
letter and we'll be most happy to introduce you around.

(a) Many of those planning to attend the show have indicated a
desire to see some of our models in operation. So we have
planned a special demonstration each day of the trade show.
Simply ask for details at our display.

3. FOLLOW-UP TO A TRADE SHOW

Your trade show exhibit may have developed a slender thread of
interest in the prospects who visited — a thread that is easily broken in
the days that follow. To enjoy maximum benefit from your trade show
investment of money and time, it's crucial that you provide for some
method for registering all visitors and initiating a follow-up contact with
them immediately after the show. One proven, successful technique is to
send a thank-you letter quickly upon completion of the show and then
have a sales rep contact the prospect shortly after that.

Model Letter 15-7

Dear _____:

Thank you for visiting our booth at the Housewares
Show. As you saw, we have many products that offer
outstanding merchandising and profit opportunities.
Some of our new products such as _____,
offer exciting growth potential. Others have long
been established in the market and have built the
name of _____ as one of quality in the mind of
the customer.

I hope you had the opportunity to see something of
our advertising plans for the year when you visited

our booth. They're exciting and offer great sales opportunities right in your own marketing area.

Enclosed are wholesale prices and catalog pages for the _____. In addition there is a 5% advertising allowance, and if your order is received before the deadlines shown on the attached sales program there are other incentives.

I have asked our Sales Representative, _____, to contact you in the next few days to answer any questions that may have come to mind since we last talked.

Sincerely,

4. LETTER OF INVITATION TO ATTEND DEALER MEETING

If your company markets through dealers, it probably holds periodic dealer meetings to announce new product lines, or to launch major advertising or sales promotion programs. Many sales organizations hold dealer training meetings. Since dealers are independent business people, getting their attendance at meetings such as these may be something of a problem. Of course, much depends on the reputation of your dealer meetings for providing benefits to the dealer that make it worthwhile to attend.

But beyond your reputation for good meetings, each meeting must be sold to the dealer organization. A letter is a good tool for introducing and selling such meetings.

Model Letter 15-8

Dear _____:

With everybody shouting it, it must be true!

19__ IS GOING TO BE THE BEST YEAR YET FOR THE _____ INDUSTRY. .

The 19__ (product name) product line is outstanding with many of the new features you have told us your customers want. Competition's eyes will bug out when they see what they're up against.

And we've been working for nine months to make sure the message gets across to your customers — a great advertising program with a new co-op program to help you get your advertising message across in your own area.

We've come up with an outstanding incentive program that will mean extra profits to you. Besides, we have a big surprise in store — a new incentive idea you're going to love.

But I can't spill all the beans now. Just make sure you come to the Dealer Annual Kick-Off Meeting. The attached sheet gives you all the lowdown. Don't miss it!

Sincerely,

Model Letter 15-9

Dear _____:

One of the frustrations of being a dealer and running a sales force is trying to find good salespeople. We realize it's been a headache.

But it's interesting to observe that while most dealers have experienced the frustration, the problem is by no means universal. Some seem to have found the answer.

We'd like to help. So we've scheduled a symposium for January 14 at _____. Just 16 dealers have been invited so the company will be select. To help us think through our mutual problem, we've asked _____, a well-respected authority on the subject of recruiting salespeople, to be with us. He'll have some ideas to contribute, but also, it will be a time of discussion . . . a chance to talk about our recruiting problems and what can be done about them. Plan to attend this important one-day session. It could be the most profitable eight hours you've spent in a long time. Just check off and mail the enclosed postcard. We'll do the rest.

Sincerely,

5. LETTER OF INVITATION TO AN OPEN HOUSE

The open house is a perennial favorite traffic-builder of businesses everywhere. And little wonder. Even its name speaks of friendly openness. Open-house events have been held for almost every imaginable occasion — new plant or office facilities, new management, a major change in product line, customer appreciation.

Whatever the reason for the open house, solid promotion of the event is the foundation of success. What better way to announce an open house than with a letter.

Model Letter 15-10

Dear _____:

You're invited to an office-warming party. You see, we've moved to our brand-new, beautiful office facility here at_____, but it will never seem like home 'til our friends have crossed its threshold. So we've set aside Friday, April 5th as a special happening. We'll have some refreshments and plenty of nice door prizes available just as an added incentive. (As if any were needed.)

Merely return the enclosed postcard to let us know to expect you. And then drop by any time from 1 to 6 p.m.

Sincerely,

Model Letter 15-11

Dear _____:

Our new 50,000 sq. ft. warehouse is now ready to serve you . . . and such service the hardware industry has never before seen. With the latest in plant layout to facilitate rapid, same-day, delivery . . . with computerized order processing and filling . . . with automated order pickup routing . . . ours is a warehouse you just must see to believe.

And that leads to the point of this letter. We would be most pleased if you would drop by anytime during the week of June 6th for a guided tour of our new warehouse facility. We're inviting you and some other of our friends and customers to see just how their orders will be quickly and accurately handled.

Just give us a ring a little in advance and plan to take about an hour. You will be pleased with what we have done and we will be pleased to have you visit us.

Sincerely,

Model Letter 15-12

Dear _____:

_____ is inviting a select group of your area's key executives to view the 19__ version of the _____ Traveling Trade Show.

Mr. Mike O'Hare, your Sales Representative for _____, will be in charge of this program which will feature _____'s newest techniques and ideas in the field of marking and labeling.

He will document his presentation with film, demonstrations, and actual product samples, drawing upon thousands of case histories in the marking and labeling field.

The showing will be held on Wednesday, April 23rd at 1:30 p.m. and will last no more than an hour and a half.

Your early response to this invitation will be appreciated. Just return the enclosed postcard.

Cordially,

16

LETTERS THAT KEEP CUSTOMERS DURING A COMPANY CRISIS

16

LETTERS THAT KEEP CUSTOMERS DURING A COMPANY CRISIS

Nothing's perfect! No matter how hard we try, something will go wrong occasionally. As a matter of fact, most companies have been through at least one crisis where something doesn't work dependably. It may be production problems, shipping problems, service difficulties. The result is the same — late deliveries, short shipments and quality problems causing headaches for the customers. And the sales manager and sales force must minimize customer dissatisfaction that results from the company's problems.

The problem usually looks even worse to those inside the company than it does to the affected customers, by the way. I recall the C.E.O. and grandson of the founder of a Fortune 500 company telling me in 1975 that he didn't know how we would ever explain to our customers that the union was going on strike at the main plant and the company might not be able to deliver as agreed on some of its current backlog of orders. The company had enjoyed over 40 years of amicable labor relations without a work stoppage or missing a delivery to customers. Their reputation for quality and dependability was unmatched in the industry, one where labor disputes resulting in plant closings was not an uncommon occurrence. But inside the company there was universal worry that the company would lose all its customers now that it was an undependable supplier. My point is not that we shouldn't be concerned, but rather that we should keep our troubles in perspective and not be afraid to explain the situation to the customer.

There is a temptation to ignore company shortcomings. Perhaps the customer won't notice the problem. Maybe we can get it corrected before it blows up in our face. Such a customer relations approach eventually will cause problems and lose customers.

We are better off to acknowledge that we have problems and assure our customers that we are doing what is necessary to solve the problems rather than waiting for the customer to complain. Not only is the customer more likely to forgive the error, but, if handled properly, they will think even more highly of the company for dealing forthrightly and doing their best to improve when they discover errors or problems.

1. EXPLAINING DELIVERY DELAYS AND SELLING THE BENEFITS OF WAITING

Strikes, temporary inventory problems, shipping delays, unexpectedly high demand for a particular product, and other circumstances beyond our control may occasionally make immediate delivery impossible. We have to reassure our sales force that the company is on top of the situation. We need to give our salespeople specific guidance on how to communicate the situation to their customers. We may also need to communicate directly with customers, smoothing the salesperson's way.

Model Letter 16-1

Dear _____:

You've undoubtedly heard the expression "nothing's perfect." Well, it turns out that expression is true. We've all enjoyed the jubilant reception our new line received in the marketplace. Demand has been so great that we are having difficulty filling all orders promptly.

Now, don't get upset. Don't forget, it beats the heck out of the alternative. For instance, right now most of our competitors can promptly fill any order they can get — because their business has been, pardon the expression, lousy.

Remember, our products are what your customer   **(a)** wants. That's why they've been buying from you right along instead of your competitor. Right now it's important for you to keep selling your accounts on the advantage of our products — to where it's worth waiting an extra week for delivery. And we can still deliver on time if they can use other products in place of the new line.

We expect the shortage situation to continue for about 90 days. Our production people are doing everything they can to catch up with demand. Hang in there — it's a temporary situation. Remember, it could be a lot worse. If the new line had bombed, you'd have no orders instead of too many, so how can we gripe because it's too much of a success?

Sincerely,

Alternate Wording:

(a) Let's count our blessings and figure out how to make the best of the situation. We need not necessarily lose any sales. First, make sure you determine exactly what your customer requires and ask yourself if certain other of our products which are readily available might not do the job as well as our newest line. Second, in those instances where only our new line will do, we simply must convince the customer that this product is worth waiting for and make the sale on a back-order basis.

Model Letter 16-2

Dear _____:

I want to thank you for the large order you just placed for our new line of _____. This line is definitely a winner and will be a fast-moving profitable item for you. You and many of our dealers were quicker and more accurate in assessing the full potential of this product in the marketplace than we were. Our initial production for this line wasn't high enough to completely fill all of the orders we received.

We have already begun increasing our production capacity. For a short period, however, we have been forced to set up an allocation system to assure fair treatment of all of our customers. **(a)**

We have shipped one-half of your order today under this system. We will ship one-fourth of your order in two weeks and the last one-fourth the week after that. By that time we expect to have the production capacity to fill all re-orders for the product immediately.

Thank you for your cooperation. I know this product will be a major contributor to your volume and profit this year. We are doing everything in our power to maximize your sales by filling your order as quickly as possible.

Sincerely,

Alternate Wording:

(a) We have already begun increasing our production capacity. For a short period, however, we will be forced to rely on a hot-line locator system for our dealers. The system is provided for new retail sales only and works this way. Just call the toll free number provided on the attached card and we will track down a unit close to you being held in stock by another dealer. All you have to do is pay freight from that store to yours. We'll handle credits and invoicing.

Model Letter 16-3

Dear _____:

After several years of uninterrupted operation, we expect a work stoppage at our central warehouse beginning next Monday. This is related to our ongoing negotiations with the labor union. We believe a mutually acceptable solution will be reached shortly.

We have made preparations to use management   **(a)**
personnel and supply you from a regional warehouse.
At this time, we expect to be able to meet your needs
completely during what we expect to be a very short
strike. We appreciate your cooperation and understanding. We expect to complete a new three-year
agreement shortly.

Sincerely,

Alternate Wording:

(a) We regret that we will not be able to make any deliveries next
week. We are confident that we will reach an amicable
settlement quickly and do not want to risk widening the gap by
doing anything the union might interpret as hostile. Moving
management personnel in to do their jobs might have that
effect. Please bear with us for this short time.

2. DELIVERY ERRORS

You never have errors and foul-ups on shipments when the
customer isn't in a hurry. It seems shipping problems only occur with
large new accounts, important customers, and accounts your salesperson
has spent extra effort on selling.

They don't care who messed up their order or how it happened.
The customer wants to know that we'll set it straight and never cause
them a problem again. This letter must tell the account what we are doing
or have done to fix our mistake. This is also an opportunity to reassure
the client that they are dealing with a company which cares for its
customers. We can also assure them that they are special customers to us
and we will make sure they receive only our best efforts in the future.

Model Letter 16-4

Dear _____:

I hope you agree with the old adage "All's well that
end's well." I found your order on the shipping dock
right after we talked. As I promised, we sent it air
freight immediately.

Once again, I apologize for the inconvenience we
caused you. It will not happen again. I checked our
procedure and found it basically sound. The Shipping

Department Manager did make several adjustments as a result of what we learned from this incident. But our freight forwarder had a new driver and we also had a new employee on the loading dock that day. A combination of coincidences resulted in the freight forwarder leaving your order on our dock and our shipping people not catching it. Our new procedure provides a final check by the supervisor, and I can therefore assure you that it won't happen again.

Thanks again for your cooperation. We appreciate your business.

Sincerely,

Model Letter 16-5

Dear _____:

My most sincere apology for shorting you on your **(a)** recent order. Our sales representative will deliver the short item when he calls next Wednesday. In the meantime we were able to dig into our packing and shipping system to determine why the error occurred. As a result we have stiffened up our final inspection procedure to preclude this type of error from recurring. I hope the gasket kits reached you in time to prevent disruption of your production schedule. The new procedures we have installed will prevent this from happening again.

Sincerely,

Alternate Wording:

(a) Everything arrived but the gasket kit! I had the requested quantity of kits sent to you special delivery as soon as you phoned.

Model Letter 16-6

Dear _____:

Haste does make waste!

As a result of our haste to insure fast delivery of your order, we attempted to deliver 12 tons of product to the lobby of your home office building. Believe me, we have learned the hard way that your home office is in Philadelphia and your manufacturing plant is in Pittsburgh.

The shipment was re-routed immediately and arrived at your plant approximately one-half day later than promised. My understanding of the situation is that your Plant Manager was worried for several hours, but that our mistake did not disrupt your production schedule.

We are paying the extra freight, of course. Frankly, **(a)** we were guilty of trying too hard to impress you with the speed of our service. This was our first chance to serve you and the order was of the highest priority. Let me assure you that we won't stop trying — and we will take that extra minute to double-check everything next time.

Sincerely,

Alternate Wording:

(a) Hopefully, we'll look back on this years from now and find it humorous. But right now I'm too embarrassed to smile, even though everything worked out without causing you great inconvenience.

3. PRODUCT RECALLS

The business humor of the times says a lot: "Ralph Nader called while you were out;" "You know it's going to be a bad week when you find the 60 Minutes television camera crew in your office Monday morning." This seems to be the age of product recalls. The media has publicized automotive product recalls most, but no industry has been immune. Integrity, complete honesty, is the most important element in communicating product problems to customers. Your Legal and Public Relations Departments or outside consultants/attorneys should have the last word. But we can still approach the situation from the positive side.

Model Letter 16-7

Dear _____:

We have learned that there is a slight chance of an electrical shock occurring to the operator of the

_____ model steam table when certain unlikely conditions are present. The attachment describes the conditions which are necessary.

There is no need to discontinue using the unit unless conditions are present as described in the attachment.

Although the chances are slight, we are taking immediate steps to correct the situation. Our representative will be calling within the next few days to add a ground wire to the unit.

We apologize for this inconvenience and promise that we will take the utmost precautions to prevent it from happening again. The safety of your workers is too important to us to be taken lightly. As a result _____ equipment is designed to be among the safest in the world.

Sincerely,

4. DISCONTINUING COMPLIMENTARY SERVICE

We know that our customers don't buy just the physical product. Rather, they buy what it will do for them. That often means the customer is buying a package of value that includes the analytical and diagnostic skills of our salesperson, the quality and dependability of the product itself, and perhaps a whole group of services such as warehousing and inventory storage and control, setup, training, as well as ongoing maintenance. But rising costs and shrinking margins seem to have been the rule for decades and appear to be for the foreseeable future. So we find ourselves taking away services we had been providing free of charge or having to add a fee for the service. Especially when our customers have come to take the extra service for granted, we must sell them on our new approach.

Model Letter 16-8

Dear _____:

We have been providing hands-on training with the three main software for your personnel each time you have purchased a computer for over three years now. The cost of providing training has been increasing steadily during that time. We know this arrangement has enabled you to get 75% productivity from an employee new to this equipment immediately and 100% within 30 days. We have struggled to keep this a complimentary service because we know how important it is to you.

Economic realities now force us to ask you for a nominal fee to partially defray the training expenses. We have almost doubled the number of hours of training provided since we started, and the methods used and materials employed have been upgraded several times. So we have increased the quality of the training, and not merely experienced an increased cost in providing the same thing we started with.   **(a)**

We believe our equipment prices are among the lowest. We do not wish to change our price structure. Rather, we believe the fair thing to do is to offer our training at a nominal fee. Your Sales Representative, Ms. Lee Ferrera, will discuss this in detail when she calls on you next week.

Sincerely,

Alternate Wording:

(a) Actually, we started out to provide a very basic software familiarization program. We have steadily increased not only the hours of instruction but the sophistication of the materials used, the quality of the instructors, and the comprehensiveness of the course. We are now providing a training course that would cost our customers a large amount if they sent their employees to a training center. Frankly, we improved the quality of our training to a level that we cannot afford to provide at no charge.

Model Letter 16-9

Dear _____:

We believe our customers appreciate our policy of offering quality merchandise at the lowest possible price. In these days of rising costs, some complimentary services which once could be provided must be discontinued.

With mixed feelings we are discontinuing our policy of free home delivery of any item purchased in our store. We will continue to offer home delivery service at a charge which defrays our cost.

Sincerely,

Model Letter 16-10

Dear _____:

Beginning the 1st of next month, we will offer our automatic inventory control service as an optional service at a small charge.

We have always taken pride in the service we provided our customers and no one else in the industry has provided an inventory control service. We continue to offer prices as low or lower than anyone in the industry. We intend to provide the highest quality product at a competitive price. We regret that rising costs no longer allow us to provide inventory control service without charge. By offering the automatic inventory service at the optional, small charge, we believe we are providing the highest quality product and service at a low price.

Sincerely,

5. REPAIRING RELATIONS WITH CUSTOMERS WHO HAVE BEEN OFFENDED BY COMPANY REPRESENTATIVES

No matter how carefully a sales manager attempts to oversee communication with valued customers, occasionally a slip-up will occur and a customer will be offended. The Sales Department's best defense against incidents which offend customers is to be familiar with all regular channels of communication and all parts of the company that may interfere with the customer. When procedures are noted that have potential for offending prospects or clients, tactful discussion with the department involved will usually provide safeguards. In large organizations, a Public Relations Manager may be on the lookout for any danger to relations with customers and will be cooperative with any suggestions from the Sales Department. But after we've done all that there will still be unfortunate incidents. Phone and face-to-face calls will often be part of your campaign to keep a customer. Letters like these will also often be part of your strategy.

Model Letter 16-11

Dear _____:

I apologize for the inconvenience we caused you last week. Our Credit Manager is also writing you to convey her regret for the mistake which held up your shipment.

The inappropriate, cold response you received when you called Monday morning was really inexcusable. That was our fault as a company. The young lady who took your call was literally brand new, first day on the job. She tells me that she was attempting to tell you, as accurately as she could, the Credit Department procedure for handling billing mistakes. She was trying to be calm and businesslike but was scared to death and that probably came across as "I don't care about your problem; this is our policy." I'm certain that she wanted to help but didn't know how, and the last thing she intended was to offend you in any way. She is now receiving training in responding to phone calls about credit problems.

A clerical error had placed your account in the 120-day column and resulted in an automatic hold on your order until the Credit Department approved shipment. We should have caught the error immediately. We're checking the procedures now and will make any adjustment necessary to assure this can't happen again.

The new credit clerk you talked to is really conscientious and wants to accompany your salesperson, Judy Sontag, on her next call at your plant to apologize in person. If it's all right with you, I'll send her out. She feels badly about offending one of our best customers. I believe she's going to be a really productive employee and I'd appreciate it if you would see her.

Thank you for your understanding. Please accept my personal apology for the inconvenience.

Sincerely,

Unless the company has made a major effort to train their service personnel to be customer-relations and sales-minded, they can occasionally irritate customers.

Model Letter 16-12

Dear _____:

You're right! Bob is outspoken, disrespectful, irascible and has the capacity to be downright obnoxious. He is also the best mechanic I have ever known. That is why I sent him out to set up your machine when time was a factor.

Bob is one of those men who seem to relate better to machines than to people. We tolerate his idiosyncrasies in the shop here because his genius with machinery is invaluable. And, frankly, I guess we've gotten used to his personality.

I apologize for the disruption I caused by sending him out. It was my mistake, and I won't include him on a service crew again.   **(a)**

Sincerely,

Alternate Wording:

(a) While we intended to get your equipment operating quickly and efficiently, we certainly didn't plan to cause such disruptions to your personnel. We've decided the best way to use Bob's expertise while curbing his tongue is to team him with a more diplomatic worker. That will be our procedure in the future.

I apologize for the disruption I caused by sending him alone to your plant last week. It won't happen again.

Humor can be very dangerous when dealing with an irate customer who has been offended by an employee of your company. However, if you know your customer well enough, and if you and your salesperson have done your part in phone and face-to-face conversations, a little humor can put an unfortunate incident in perspective and get you back to the jovial, day-to-day repartee you enjoyed previously.

Model Letter 16-13

Dear _____:

I want to apologize for the letter mistakenly sent to you by our Credit Department. You have every right to be upset with us.

I offer you the choice of one of the following methods of reparation:

(Check one — just one)

☐ Let me off the hook and accept my sincere apology.

☐ Insist I fire the clerk in our Credit Department who sent the letter. (His name is Bob Cratchit and he has a son named Tiny Tim. He is very sorry about the mistake.)

☐ I will report to your office at 8:00 a.m. Monday and you may hit me in the face with a pie. (This was suggested by your salesman who offered to drive me over.)

Seriously, when I allow an embarrassing mistake like this to happen, especially to as valued and prompt-paying an account as you, it is unforgivable. It won't happen again.

Sincerely,

6. WHEN AN ACCOUNT IS WITHOUT A SALES OR SERVICE REPRESENTATIVE

If you are doing your sales management job effectively, your customers come to depend upon your sales reps, see them as trusted advisors, helpers. So when you lose a salesperson or a service representative unexpectedly, your customers may feel they have lost part of what they are buying from your company. If customers are not assured that their needs will continue to be satisfied during the period they are without a sales or service representative, they will take their business elsewhere.

Model Letter 16-14

Dear _____ :

When we talked the other day I promised to have a sales executive to replace Greg Nelson within a short time and I assured you someone would be taking care of you in the short interim period. Ms. Dorothy Ogden will contact you within a day or two. You will find her knowledgeable and capable and totally concerned with providing your company, and your Engineering Department in particular, with not only product, but also the lab services and consulting you are used to. Ms. Ogden has been the Sales Engineer in the adjoining county for three years and her customers feel she is indispensable. She has a BSEE degree from Georgia Tech and her master's from Purdue.

I expect to be ready to permanently assign a new Sales Engineer within six weeks. Don't let your people get too attached to Ogden during the next six weeks. I guarantee your new Sales Engineer will be the same caliber.

Sincerely,

Model Letter 16-15

Dear _____ :

Please consider me as your sales representative for the next 30 days. As you know, Jack left us unexpectedly. We intend to continue providing you with a professional representative to serve your needs and are presently considering several highly qualified people.   **(a)**

In the meantime, you are stuck with me. Please phone me at XXX-XXXX (direct line) when I can be of service. Two of our best salespeople, Dick Montney and Brenda Sanchez, will be helping me serve your needs. The three of us will do our best for you.   **(b)**

I promise you that the care we are taking in selecting your new sales representative will make the short wait worthwhile.

Thanks for your cooperation.

Sincerely,

Alternate Wording:

(a) Please consider Bill Caldwell as your sales representative for the next 30 days.

(b) We have relieved Bill of some of his other responsibilities so he can provide you with the care you deserve. When you need his service you can contact him at XXX-XXXX. In the meantime you can expect him to make calls at your office with the same frequency as did Jack.

Good service people can develop a rapport with an account and become as indispensable as a sales rep — dare we say even more indispensable — on occasion. We must assure the account that the company will continue to provide top quality service.

Model Letter 16-16

Dear _____:

Sam Wilkins has resigned from his position of Service Engineer and will be leaving us in two weeks.

We are assigning two neighboring Service Engineers, Curtis Johnson and Brian Engel, to service your equipment until a permanent replacement is assigned. We are assigning two men to assure that you will not have to wait for service. Please call Jim Bloss, the Service Manager, or me whenever you need a Service Engineer. Jim or I will see that you receive prompt service.

We hope to have a permanent Service Engineer assigned to you within 30 days. Thank you for your cooperation during this interim period. I promise you that the care we are taking in selecting your new Service Engineer will make the short wait worthwhile.

Sincerely,

Model Letter 16-17

Dear _____:

By the time you read this letter you will probably have heard about the automobile mechanic's strike. The dealers association will make every effort to resolve the situation quickly and fairly. In the meantime, my main concern is that you are able to obtain any service you may require on your 19XX_____ automobile.

I have attached a list of dealers outside of this area who will not be affected by the strike and also a list of local service stations and garages who have competent mechanics and adequate facilities to deal with normal maintenance. Please phone me personally at XXX-XXXX (direct line) if you have any extraordinary service need and I will personally see that your needs are satisfied.

We expect this situation to be remedied in a short time. I will personally do everything I can to assure that you will not be inconvenienced.

Thank you for working with us.

Sincerely,

17

LETTERS THAT PRODUCE NEW BUSINESS FROM LOST ACCOUNTS

17

LETTERS THAT PRODUCE
NEW BUSINESS FROM
LOST ACCOUNTS

The lost sales account is part of life for every sales organization. No matter how hard you try, some customer loss must be expected. Buyers die. Personalities clash. Mistakes sometimes occur. Better opportunities seem provided by competition.

Even though you may have lost the account, you may possess considerable advantage over your competition should the lost account ever become available again. You probably understand the lost account's business better than competition. You may know people in the organization better and may have some level of rapport that is lacking by a competitive sales organization. The lost customer knows your sales organization and service reputation. He knows your reputation for product quality and your reliability. Even though you may have fallen down in one or more of these areas, some pluses probably remain in the prospect's mind. Mending fences may be easier than building new business with a prospect totally unfamiliar with your organization.

Certainly a personal sales call is the most forceful method for regaining a lost account. But every means should be used to keep your company name before the lost account and mend bridges.

So the letter has value in regaining such business. Many managers program a continuous mail campaign to keep their company name before the lost account and reinforce the positive reasons the lost account should again do business with them.

To be successful such a direct mail campaign with the lost account should:

- Be programmed on a regular basis. When changing accounts the customer most likely went immediately with a competitor. Getting the customer back may require that you send periodic letters until such time that conditions are ripe for the customer to once more make a move. Such a letter program will keep your name before the customer and tell him that you value his business.

- Be closely tailored to show correction of the problem that caused him to break the relationship. If you are aware of the reason you lost the customer, refer to correction of that condition in your letter. If you don't know why you lost the customer, you will need to use a more general approach. Or perhaps you can use a probing letter as in Model Letter 17-3.

The letters which follow are provided in categories according to the appeal used to secure the customer's interest.

1. AN APPEAL ON THE BASIS OF PAST RELATIONSHIP

Even when a customer is no longer buying from your company, there may remain some feeling of relationship that can reactivate a buying status. Perhaps the customer has just drifted away. Or perhaps a competitor has made an offer that temporarily seems more attractive. As long as the reason is not great, a simple "we've missed you" letter may get the customer on the buying list again. Such is the following letter.

Model Letter 17-1

Dear _____:

We Miss You!

Yes, every one of our customers is important to us.

And we take special note when they haven't bought from us for a time.

It's been several months since you made a purchase **(a)** from _____ Maybe the reason has been small, or big. But won't you come back? We miss you!

Sincerely,

Alternate Wording:

(a) You have not purchased from us in several months. Whatever the reason, we want to do whatever is necessary to earn your business. We miss you!

If yours is a retail business that uses its own charge acount system, you will be able to locate inactive customers from idle charge accounts. This letter can tell these inactives you miss them.

Model Letter 17-2

Dear _____:

You haven't used your _____ charge account for some time. That means you may be missing some tremendous values.

You will always find special values at _____. And your charge account is an especially convenient way to take advantage of them.

Stop in soon, won't you? Our charge account customers are especially valued. And we'll show it.

Sincerely,

When the customer strays, the reason may be unknown to you or the sales rep. This letter probes for the reason. It makes a light, easy-to-read method for learning the nature of a problem.

Model Letter 17-3

Dear _____:

It's been some time since you've bought from us and that grieves us terribly. If we goofed, please give us a chance to correct it. Just check off why and return this letter in the enclosed, addressed envelope. Maybe we can help out.

☐ We haven't needed to replenish inventory lately. We'll be ordering again sometime soon.

☐ Have your sales rep call. We'd like to place an order.

☐ Yes, you goofed. But tell your sales rep to call. Maybe we can work it out.

☐ No, we haven't ordered and here is the reason. _____

_____

Thanks! We appreciate your candid comments.

Sincerely,

2. AN APPEAL BASED ON A CHANGE IN PERSONNEL

An appeal to the inactive customer to buy once again from your company is most likely to be effective when closely related to the cause of the separation. For those customers who drifted away because of friction with some member of your organization, these letters are valuable.

Model Letter 17-4

Dear _____:

We've put on a new service face . . . new service **(a)** manager . . . new service organization. All to serve you better.

It's been some time since you bought from us. Won't you give us a try? You'll be pleased with the changes you find.

Sincerely,

Alternate Wording:

(a) We have a brand-new organization ready to serve you. Your new sales representative will be calling on you soon to see how we can meet your needs. Our new service manager has built a capable service team to serve you better than ever before.

Model Letter 17-5

Dear _____:

The new broom sweeps clean. And we intend to prove it's so.

Hello! I've just been appointed sales manager for _____. We plan to prove ourselves to you by making the changes in our organization you've been asking for. We think you'll be pleased with our new face. _____, your sales representative, tells me it has been some time since you have placed an order with us. He also tells me he is firmly convinced that the changes we have made will open the door to a new relationship between us. He plans to call you this week for an appointment to explain our new policies and programs to you.

In addition, I will be calling you for an appointment to meet you personally.

Sincerely,

3. AN APPEAL BASED ON REVISED POLICIES

When old policies have caused a lost customer, this letter may serve to reactivate the account.

Model Letter 17-6

Dear _____:

We've made a change in our organization we think you'll like.

The size of our sales representative territories has **(a)** been reduced to permit more frequent calls on our customers and more individualized attention to your needs. You can expect a call from the _____ representative on alternate weeks now. As a result you can expect fewer special orders and less time between deliveries. _____ will be calling on you Tuesday, March 5th and on alternate Tuesday's thereafter. She will be happy to help you inventory your stock and prepare an order.

Sincerely,

Alternate Wording:

(a) We have introduced a new credit policy which includes cash discounts and other favorable terms which we believe will be of interest to you. We also now offer an inventory service which could reduce your present investment in stock.

4. AN APPEAL BASED ON A NEW PRODUCT

Occasionally you may be unable to satisfy a customer's unusual needs from your standard line. When a product later becomes available which will meet the customer's needs, you will want to so advise him. Although the sales rep will have the primary responsibility for notifying the customer of the new product, a letter from you will assist the sales rep to prepare the customer.

Model Letter 17-7

Dear _____:

Last year you provided us with a challenge we were unable to meet. We were unable to provide you with a sprayer nozzle to handle your plastic film application. That doesn't often happen. As we talked with other companies with similar manufacturing applications, we became aware of a new marketing opportunity.

Our Engineering Department loves challenges, and did they ever respond to the one you provided them. We think our new Model 620B sprayer nozzle will meet precisely the needs you described earlier.

Our Sales Representative, _____, will be calling you this week for an appointment to describe and demonstrate this new product.

Sincerely,

Here is another letter with an appeal based on changed product specifications. In this case the customer had quit dealing with the company because the product was not meeting the needs to which it was placed.

Model Letter 17-8

Dear _____:

Losing a valued customer is a most painful experience. And when you lose the customer because the product fails to meet the requirements to which it is placed, the experience is enough to cause one to give up selling. (Almost!) I really took the loss of your business to heart. As a result I appealed to our engineering staff to improve the flash point of our 602 cutting fluid to a point that would meet your specifications. As a result we now have a newly designed cutting fluid that has not only a much improved flash point but several other improved characteristics as well. The big advantage of our improved cutting fluid is that it will meet the cutting lubricant needs of your total department thus reducing your inventory investment and storage space requirements.

Thank you for calling this need to our attention. Why don't you give our new cutting fluid a trial run. I'll drop around next week to answer your questions and to set up a delivery for that purpose.

Sincerely,

5. AN APPEAL BASED ON A SPECIAL SALE

Perhaps only inertia is keeping the customer from initiating a purchase. Many products are bought on a discretionary basis. The customer may buy or delay depending on a sense of priorities at the moment. Getting the customer to buy requires a special reason to act now. Here is a letter that is designed to jolt the procrastinator into action.

Model Letter 17-9

Dear _____:

Would you believe that 24 months have passed since you bought your (model car) from us? It's about now that many of our customers begin to think about a new model.

We'd like to encourage you to come in to see the 19___   **(a)**
model _____. To do that I've enclosed a
coupon worth a free lubrication and oil change on
me. And while your car is in for servicing, I'll give
your car an appraisal for trade-in on a 19___ While
you're waiting maybe you would like to take a look at
and test drive a beautiful (model).

Just call me and I'll set up an appointment with our   **(b)**
service people. That way you can be sure of taking
only a minimum time to get your car serviced.

Sincerely,

Alternate Wording:

(a) We'd like you to experience many new features, increased gas
mileage, and responsiveness of the 19___ To accomplish that I
would like to lend you my own new _____ for a full day
next Saturday. When you pick up my car I'll give your car an
appraisal for trade-in on a 19___ Used car prices have been
increasing and you may be pleasantly surprised.

(b) I'll phone you Wednesday to confirm this arrangement. I know
you'll enjoy driving the 19___ _____ as much as I do.

6. AN APPEAL BASED ON NEW EXPERTISE

Some products and many services are sold only with considerable
backup experience. This experience is an added feature that accompanies
the sale to make the product of greater value to the customer. The sale of
some products and services is so heavily dependent on such backup
expertise that a sale is difficult without it. When new experience is
acquired, new sales opportunities are opened up. Here is a model letter
that was written on such an occasion. Although not a dead account, this
situation represents business that may be newly available.

Model Letter 17-10

Dear _____:

We have been providing many of your banking
services for some time and we're mighty proud of it.
However, we have not yet been able to convince you
to use our payroll processing program. That may be
understandable when you consider that at the time

we last talked to you about it, we had no direct experience in your unique industry or union situation.

But now we have considerable experience . . . not only in the same industry in which you are involved but with the same union. In fact, we believe our experience with other similar companies will be invaluable to you as you consider our payroll processing system for your own company.

Like to hear more about how our payroll system has worked for these other companies . . . How it has saved them money and time and has provided them with the reports they require when they need them?

I'll call you next Monday for an appointment.

Sincerely,

18

LETTERS THAT PUT CUSTOMERS AND INFLUENTIAL THIRD PARTIES ON YOUR SALES TEAM

18

LETTERS THAT PUT CUSTOMERS AND INFLUENTIAL THIRD PARTIES ON YOUR SALES TEAM

The letters in this chapter will help you produce tangible, immediate results in the form of additional sales to new prospects, support of outside influences who can sway a sale, and increased loyalty to your company and products by present customers.

Potential sales aids are all around you. Satisfied customers, influential experts in a science or industry, and financial institutions which make purchase of your product possible can become valuable assets for producing additional sales. Usually a powerful new sales tool is a sizeable budget item. Well, this is a productive sales tool that costs nothing but a little "sweat equity." A bit of sales skill, a letter requesting assistance, and perhaps a lunch or other appropriate social gesture of thank you, are the cost of a sales aid money can't buy.

Your satisfied customers can be one of your most valuable assets for producing additional sales. Their testimony on your behalf can be the difference in a tough sale. There may be influential experts in your market whose opinion of your product can sway the purchaser. If your product is "bigger than a bread box," financially at least, a large ticket item dependent upon outside financing, the good will of the finance source or banker can be invaluable. If you can convince the finance people your product produces positive cash flow and makes money, their receptive attitude toward financing your product can be the difference on many sales that could go either way. And if you are selling package goods or consumer durables to the entire population, promotional activities featuring satisfied customers can bring you and your product favorable publicity and additional sales.

1. REQUESTING CUSTOMER TESTIMONIALS

Prospects will pay more attention to what your customers say about your product than they do to what you say. Testimonials from satisfied customers can be powerful sales tools. We can be more certain of obtaining cooperation from satisfied customers if we:

- Explain exactly what help we want from them.
- Make it simple and easy for them to comply with our request.
- Thank them for their help in specific ways.

One caution in regard to thanking customers for their help: sales managers who have been successful in securing customer testimonials agree that small and thoughtful "thank yous" are most appropriate and insure future cooperation. A thank you letter or phone call, an occasional lunch or invitation to a ball game, or whatever appropriate social event, are effective — but large gifts can appear to be bribes and can insult the integrity of the satisfied customer.

Model Letter 18-1

Dear _____:

Thanks again for your hospitality the other day. I enjoyed touring your efficient, well-run production facility. It's easy to see how your company maintains the reputation for quality that you have earned over the years. I was pleased to see the part our products play in maintaining the high standards you set for your finished product. I appreciated your comments concerning our company as a dependable supplier of consistently high quality components. Quite frankly, I'd like to quote you because I know your opinion would be respected by similar companies in other industries.

My public relations people tell me I need your formal permission to quote you, although you assured me it would be all right with you the other day. I'll phone in a couple of days to request a meeting with you and our public relations manager to "formally" request your permission to refer to you and your company in our sales materials. Thanks again for your comments and cooperation.

Sincerely,

Model Letter 18-2

Dear _____:

Our company is proud to be your supplier. We **(a)** appreciate your business over the years, and we appreciate your compliments on our quality and service. I want to ask you for a favor. You are a very well-known and highly regarded company. Your opinion carries a lot of weight with many prospective accounts we are calling on. I am asking your permission to quote you as a satisfied customer. Specifically, would you be willing to send me a short **(b)** note telling me:

- How we have been able to help save time and money in your operation.
- What kind of job we have done for you (dependability and service).
- Any comments you care to make.

I hope I'm not being too presumptuous. Your experiences would be most helpful to us in presenting our product and service to buyers in other industries (not competitors of your company).

A pre-addressed, stamped envelope is enclosed. I'll phone in a day or two to discuss and answer any questions.

Sincerely,

Alternate Wording:

(a) I want to ask a favor which will only take a few minutes.

(b) If I'm not taking too much for granted, would you be willing to drop me a note telling me in what way our product has been most helpful to you? Your opinion concerning ways our product has helped cut costs and increase productivity would be appreciated.

Model Letter 18-3

Dear _____:

I enjoyed visiting with you the other day. I am happy to know that you have been pleased with the service we provide.

May I have your permission to refer to you and your company when discussing our product with other companies? As you know, many buyers are interested in the experiences of others when they are purchasing from a supplier for the first time. Your company's high standards are well-known and respected. Rest assured that we will provide the same satisfaction to these new accounts that we have provided you.

Sincerely,

Don't forget a formal "thank you" every once in a while to those special customers who have consented to provide testimonials. It's easy to forget and take them for granted once they've agreed to help.

Model Letter 18-4

Dear _____:

This is an anniversary of sorts. About a year ago you agreed to do me the favor of appearing in our sales brochure as a reference to our quality and service.

I wanted to let you know that my salespeople have commented many times during the year how favorably prospects are impressed by your testimony to our dependability. You are widely known and your opinion is respected. Again, I appreciate your help very much. If I can ever be of assistance in any way please don't hesitate to ask. We value the special relationship between our two firms and want it to continue for many, many years.

Sincerely,

The sales manager who provided the following letter represents a product which is difficult to demonstrate and visualize except in existing installations. This is a request to actually "tour" prospects to the satisfied customer's facility. This can be a potent sales tool even with products which can be visualized and demonstrated in simpler ways.

Model Letter 18-5

Dear _____:

I've been thinking about your company ever since my visit last week and have decided to ask you for a favor.

You know how difficult our product is to describe to someone who is not already using it. However, when prospects observe it in use, they can't help but be impressed with the obvious quality, efficiency, and economy. Well, I would like to use your operation as an example with a company currently considering us. Would you allow me to bring them over to tour your facility? I want to do this at a time most convenient to you and will be careful not to disrupt your operation in any way. I would appreciate it if you would personally act as our guide. I will be sure to absent myself for a few minutes during the tour to insure that my prospective customers feel free to discuss our product with you in private.

I will phone you later this week to discuss this proposed tour. I'm proud you and your company are customers and believe our product speaks for itself when observed in your operation.

(a)

If this project will fit into your schedule without inconveniencing you, I'll certainly appreciate it.

Sincerely,

Alternate Wording:

(a) As you know, one of the most important benefits our customers receive by using our product is the ease and efficiency with which it is integrated with allied equipment. But unfortunately that's a benefit that must be seen to be appreciated.

This letter is sent after a tour to thank the customer for visitation privileges. Notice that in this case the writer was able to point out specific benefits the customer had received by allowing the sales manager to tour the facility.

Model Letter 18-6

Dear _____:

My thanks again for allowing me to tour your facility last Tuesday with a group of potential customers. They were enthusiastic about our product as a result of the tour and two orders have already been placed. They were also impressed with the efficiency of your **(a)** entire operation and with your attention to quality control. As you mentioned to me on Tuesday, several of them did represent companies who should be prospects for your product. I'll be glad to pass along this information to your sales force. Thanks again for your hospitality and cooperation.

I'd like to come over next week and discuss the possibility of doing this again sometime in the future if you agree this project was advantageous to both of our companies.

Sincerely,

Alternate Wording:

(a) They were also impressed with your modern operation and particularly with the efficiency with which the plant is laid out. You must be very proud of what you have been able to accomplish and deservedly so. Please accept my personal thanks and also the thanks of those who visited your plant. You have benefited not only me, but also those who may be able to utilize our equipment as you have.

2. SEEKING OUTSIDE FINANCING

When you are in business you never have enough cash. This homily was not taken from *Inc.* magazine's small business philosophy. Rather, you will hear some form of this expression anywhere business people gather. And it is definitely not confined to "small-" and medium-sized business; the largest companies also could always use more financing. Remember Chrysler Corporation and government guarantees for loans to get the money it takes to make money. By the same token, if you are selling a large ticket item, capital equipment business-to-business, or consumer durables to a mass market, you can never have too much financing available for your customers. Many marketeers actively solicit banks and commercial finance companies as finance sources for their product. The buyer still must be qualified but it smooths the way when the finance source is already familiar with your product and sees it as a wise investment.

Model Letter 18-7

Dear _____:

Your firm is well-known and highly regarded as a primary source of financing by the accounts my company services. Your reputation for fair dealing and business sense makes your firm the first choice of many of the best manufacturers my sales force calls on when a capital investment is being considered.

For this reason, I believe it would be of mutual benefit for us to meet. The equipment of XXXXXX Corp. is the standard of excellence in material handling in the Scandinavian countries and most of western Europe. We have become quite well-known and highly regarded among industrial engineers and material handling experts in North America, but we are not yet quite a household word. Users of our equipment are enthusiastic about the dependability, low maintenance, and cost savings they have experienced. Less obviously quantifiable, but even more exciting to some of our customers, is the flexibility they gain in configuring the manufacturing floor.

But you almost have to see it for yourself and hear the manufacturing managers describe what our equipment has done for their plant to appreciate its soundness as a capital equipment investment. I'd like to see you next Wednesday or Thursday and briefly discuss our product and show you pictures of a couple of installations. If the efficiencies we describe are appealing to you, I'd be glad to arrange for a visit to some progressive local manufacturers using our equipment so you can see for yourself.

I'll call in a day or two to arrange an appointment for us to meet.

Sincerely,

3. PROMOTIONAL ACTIVITIES FEATURING CUSTOMERS

Particularly if you sell a consumer item, you have the opportunity to feature customers in your promotional activities. The following letter emphasizes a product value and, in addition, is a good public relations effort with a popular appeal to the local news media as a humorous human interest story. Although this promotional activity was submitted by a successful marketer of a consumer good, with a little imagination the general concept might be used even with heavy industrial goods if an interesting and newsworthy presentation to a customer is included.

Model Letter 18-8

Dear _____:

Congratulations for helping to prove there's always room for one more in a Volkswagen. We would like to present you and your husband with a savings bond which we hope will be used toward your son's education.

Since 19__, when we started the Bonds-for-Babies program, we have awarded savings bonds to 302 children. We are making arrangements with your dealer and area distributor to present this bond to you. I am sure you will be hearing from them shortly.

Meanwhile, I hope you will enjoy driving your

Volkswagen for a long time to come — even if you never again have a trip as eventful as the one of May 10!

Sincerely,

4. RESPONDING TO CONSUMER QUESTIONS

If you are selling to a broad market of consumers, you may occasionally receive inquiries or questions from concerned consumers or consumer activist groups. These inquiries are not to be handled lightly, and your company may have a policy and procedure for responding to them (see Chapter 19).

The following letter is included only to show that such inquiries can be opportunities for positive communication and can result in more understanding of the value of the product or service and greater customer satisfaction. It is a classic PR response letter.

Model Letter 18-9

Dear _____ :

Thanks for stating your concerns about Ohio Bell's advertising and Hello. These questions certainly are warranted, and I welcome the opportunity to explain why we use such communication tools to reach you and other customers with information about how to make the best use of your telephone service. First, to your specific question — the cost of Hello. Each Hello is produced for about ½¢ per customer and it rides along postage-free on the bill envelope. Every month it reaches about $2\frac{1}{3}$ million customers who rate it above television, radio, and newspapers in providing them useful information about their service.

Your suggestion that the elimination of Hello and advertising would cut expenses and benefit customers is understandable. Unfortunately, such an expense reduction would increase your telephone bill — not decrease it. Ohio Bell spends this money to communicate with customers for three reasons: 1. To improve employee and equipment efficiency by telling customers how to use the telephone properly; 2. to increase revenue through sales such as long distance and extensions; 3. to help customers get more value out of their service. Here are some examples of how advertising and Hello benefit you and Ohio Bell.

- We encourage you to use your directory rather than call an information operator to locate numbers — that holds down people and equipment costs.

- We suggest that customers dial long distance calls themselves rather than using an operator — that saves you money and cuts expenses at the same time. A recent Bell System study shows that $100 is saved in operating costs for every $1 spent to advertise customer dialing of long distance calls.

- We pass along dozens of tips about the proper use of your telephone, especially through Hello — customers who follow this information ad get more value from their telephone.

- We advertise to sell more optional telephone services like extensions, Trimline, and Princess which increase revenue. Revenue produced in this manner decreases the amount that we have to ask to offset the effects of inflation.

Despite this evidence, you may continue to feel there is something wrong about the telephone company spending money to advertise. You can be sure we will continue explaining why this benefits both the company and its customers. I prefer to respond to this concern rather than the one which you and all customers and shareholders would raise if we were to discontinue use of these communication tools. Then we would be accused of irresponsible management action for ignoring opportunities to save money. Against that charge, I would have no defense.

I hope this answers your questions. If you would like to discuss it, please let me know.

Sincerely,

19

WHEN NOT
TO WRITE LETTERS

19

WHEN NOT
TO WRITE LETTERS

Even in this age of communication satellites and electronic communication wonders, it is difficult to imagine conducting business without letters. The value of letters in conveying ideas is unchallenged. Yet, on occasion, a letter may not be the most appropriate means to express your idea. We have mentioned several such instances in previous chapters. This chapter is devoted completely to such considerations.

1. WHEN PERSONAL CONTACT IS MORE EFFECTIVE

Face-to-face or telephone communication possess certain strengths over the written word. For example, consider these occasions when the spoken word may be more effective:

- *When confidentiality is important.* Certain messages are for the receiver only. Should others read your letter, embarrassment, competitive advantage, or other problems might occur.

295

For example, severe discipline problems should be handled personally. One important reason for this personal touch is that no one should know of the discipline action other than you and the salesperson. Confidentiality is generally also important where newly developed products are involved. Many companies restrict their use of letters concerning new products or marketing ideas until they are sufficiently well-developed to assure that competition will not be able to secure a competitive edge with the product or idea.

Of course, one solution to the public quality of the letter is to mark it "personal and confidential," which is still done in many companies. This technique seems to work reasonably well at least to keep the letter from being read by anyone other than the intended reader until they have the opportunity. The problem occurs when such letters are not handled with sufficient care at the receiving or sending end and prying eyes learn of their content after the receiver. Generally, though, the best solution is to refrain from any letter that you wouldn't want prying eyes to read.

- *When body and facial responses are an important part of the message to be transmitted.* Some time ago the term "Body Language" was made popular as the means of determining what others are thinking by reading their body stances. We have all learned that certain facial expressions have special meaning to us. There is little doubt that we stand to learn more of the delicate meaning of the speaker and they of ours when personal, face-to-face talk is involved. Although such finely tuned communication is not always required, when it is we should opt for the personal style that provides it.

  For example, discussing a drinking problem may require face-to-face contact, not only for the personal nature of the problem but also to provide you with the opportunity to read subtle body expressions. The employee looking away when promising to reform may tell you more than words can convey.

- *To emphasize the importance of the message.* Whenever you wish to convey urgency or great importance, the spoken word, particularly face-to-face, is generally most effective. Making a special trip across town or to the next state has a way of conveying the message that whatever it is the speaker has to say must be of great importance. The salesperson who knows the boss is making a special trip to talk is alerted to the meeting's importance. The customer who receives a personal call from the sales manager knows the manager feels the call is important and, in addition, senses the importance with which the manager holds the customer.

2. WHEN IT'S IMPORTANT NOT TO COMMIT THE COMPANY

Letters can have a way of becoming official doctrine or law. This is especially true where union or activist groups are concerned. If you don't mean to commit the company to a particular point of view and you are writing to someone who intentionally or otherwise might misconstrue the meaning of your letter, best use the spoken word. Here are some examples:

- *Use the spoken word when a letter might be construed as a contract.* When you are dealing with salespeople or customers in sensitive areas and when you are not completely sure of your ground, it is better not to communicate in writing — for instance, in a dispute over commissions or terms of employment. Written communication should be avoided unless you are willing to have the terms provided in the letter bind the company as a legal contract.

  If you deal with a union, you have probably already found that you must always be sensitive to what you commit to writing unless you fully intend to obligate the company.

  The same can be true with customers. Pricing is often a delicate area, especially where prices must be negotiated with the customer. Again, written comments to the customer concerning price should not be made unless you intend to bind the company with your statement.

- *Resist writing letters when social action groups are attempting to trap or entice the company.* "Corporate gadfly" was once the term. "Consumer activist" is the popular label used today for the groups and individuals who question and criticize the way businesses are run.

  What response should a sales manager make to inquiries or criticisms from consumer or social action groups? In many instances, the answer is no response and particularly no written response. A small and seemingly insignificant comment made to an activist group can mushroom into a newsworthy item which can do great harm to your company's image and your sales.

When a written reply is made to such a group, it should be with the counsel of your Legal Department. They can assist you with the precise wording of your letter and can save the company much anguish. You may be well-advised to never reply to an individual concerning a social or activist issue, and only to those groups which have established some reputation in the community. Some groups are formed on a shoestring, exist for a short while to harrass a few companies, and dissolve again with little accomplished other than to leave the public with considerable false impressions. If you have not heard of the group, don't reply either orally or in writing until you have determined its legitimacy through the local newspaper or government agency.

Good advice is to consign such correspondence to a specialized department within your company. Special training is often required and when used can frequently turn a company problem into an asset. The letter included in Chapter 18, page 291 is an example.

3. WHEN TIMELINESS IS ESSENTIAL

Two-, three-day, and up to one-week delivery by the postal service is a common expectancy today. Slow mail deliveries can seriously hamper any communication dependent on timely expression of your thoughts to your reader. If speed is important, better use a telephone.

- *Use a telephone when customer satisfaction requires rapid handling.* When a customer problem occurs, speed is important. Take two or three days required for a letter and the customer will perceive the delay as a lack of interest on your part. If you should require any additional information from the customer, the handling of a customer complaint can run into weeks. That's a good lesson in how to lose a valuable customer.

The personal touch is most valuable when customer complaints are involved. Not only what the customer says, but how he or she says it can be determined. And frequently the time required to work out the problem is reduced to minutes rather than days.

If a direct, personal meeting is impractical due to the distance involved, the telephone provides the next best method for resolving customer complaints. Although the telephone deprives us of some of the benefits of a face-to-face talk, it does convey the importance we place on the handling of the matter and does speed up the handling. Whether handling the customer's problem involves a face-to-face talk or telephone, a letter can provide effective follow-up as described in Chapter 12.

• *The letter is not best for daily direction of the sales force.* The essence of the sales manager's job, to make salespeople the best they can be, is better accomplished with face-to-face or telephone conversation. Daily direction requires close timing and quick feedback. Send a letter to direct a salesperson to make a timely call on a prospect, and competition may already have secured the account by the time your letter arrives.

Day-to-day coaching is difficult to accomplish by letter. Coaching requires personal observation of how the salesperson is performing. It requires personal give-and-take to arrive at an awareness of key problems and the most effective solution.

All of the points made in this chapter on when not to write letters, of course are just common sense. Perhaps the most important common-sense rule is one that if followed would make all of the other ones unheeded. The general rule is to match the communication tool to the job to be accomplished. Just keep in mind that the letter allows less room for misinterpretation, but is less personal and less timely. The telephone or personal call can provide a greater sense of urgency and importance.